REJOICING
in
LAMENT

REJOICING in LAMENT

Wrestling with Incurable Cancer & Life in Christ

J. TODD BILLINGS

BrazosPress

a division of Baker Publishing Group
Grand Rapids, Michigan

Published by Brazos Press
a division of Baker Publishing Group
P.O. Box 6287, Grand Rapids, MI 49516-6287
www.brazospress.com

Printed in the United States of America

Library of Congress Cataloging-in-Publication Data
Billings, J. Todd.
    Rejoicing in lament : wrestling with incurable cancer and life in Christ /J. Todd Billings.
        pages cm
    Includes bibliographical references and index.
    ISBN 978-1-58743-358-0 (pbk.)
    1. Cancer—Patients—Religious life. 2. Cancer—Religious aspects—Christianity. 3. Suffering—Religious aspects—Christianity. 4. Billings, J. Todd. I. Title.
BV4910.33.B55 2015
248.8′6196994—dc23   2014040099

15 16 17 18 19 20 21   7 6 5 4 3 2 1

To those who cry out to the Lord amidst the fog

Contents

Preface   ix

Acknowledgments   xiii

Abbreviations   xv

1. Walking in the Fog: A Narrowed Future or a Spacious Place?   1

2. Sorting through the Questions: The Book of Job, the Problem of Evil, and the Limits of Human Wisdom   17

3. Lamenting in Trust: Praying with the Psalmist amid a Sea of Emotions   35

4. Lamenting to the Almighty: Discerning the Mystery of Divine Providence   55

5. Joining the Resistance: Lament and Compassionate Witness to the Present and Future King   75

6. Death in the Story of God and in the Church   93

7. Praying for Healing and Praying for the Kingdom   111

8. In the Valley: Toxins, Healing, and Strong Medicine for Sinners   131

Contents

9. The Light of Perfect Love in the Darkness: God's Impassible Love in Christ   149

10. "I Am Not My Own": Our Story Incorporated into Christ's   169

Notes   191

Preface

Before my blood cancer diagnosis in September 2012, I never anticipated that I would write a book like this. This book was written during various stages of my cancer treatment process; that process has not ended but continues with chemotherapy as I write this preface now. Some sections of the book were written in the hospital. Other parts were written while I was in quarantine from public places because of a compromised immune system after a stem cell transplant. All of it was written amid the physical and emotional turmoil derived from both my cancer treatments and my new prospects as someone diagnosed with an incurable cancer at the age of thirty-nine.

In the first chapter, I describe the basic structure and format of the book and the way in which I intertwine my cancer story with the exploration of a much weightier story—the story of God's saving action in and through Jesus Christ. I intend for that chapter to be the introduction to the book. But by way of preface, I would like to add a few comments about the background, genre, and intended audience of the book.

After my diagnosis, I prayerfully immersed myself in Scripture, especially the Psalms. New biblical and theological questions were becoming urgent. Since my diagnosis took place in the middle of a sabbatical semester of research and writing, I had the time and space to turn my attention to biblical and theological works that pursue these questions as I began chemotherapy. I was able to temporarily set aside some of my earlier plans for the sabbatical in order to do this. Quite naturally, some of my new reflections made their way onto my medical blog on CarePages.com.[1] And eventually, as chapter 1 narrates, I heeded the advice of those around me to expand my reflections into a book. I wrote the book not only for others but also as a part of my own process of coming before the presence of God in my new life after the diagnosis. I decided to honestly take on the tough theological and existential questions rather than dodge them. They are the questions that I live with. And frequently, they are the questions that other Christians who have experienced loss live with as well. There is an urgency underlying this book that is analogous to one that many viewers experienced in the 2013 movie *Gravity*. Dr. Ryan Stone, in desperate conditions, says it this way: "I know, we're all gonna die. But I'm gonna die today." I do not have the burden of an expectation of imminent death. But I do have an urgency to cut through to the most pressing questions with a different sort of expectation—a medical expectation that my death is likely to come much sooner than previously expected, that my hopes toward the future cannot be what they used to be. This is a loss not just for me but for my family, for my friends, for my community of faith. How does this sudden loss, which sinks in gradually, relate to the abundant life that we enjoy in Christ? Does Scripture give us the "answer" to our pressing questions about *why* this is happening, or does God give us something different—even better—than that through Scripture? How do the psalms of lament, the book of Job, and the New Testament witness to Jesus Christ and life in him testify to the loving power of the Triune God? The most potent questions, when one pushes deeply enough, are ultimately not about our experience but about the story of God made known in Jesus Christ.

While I explored these questions as a scholar in my reading and later in my writing, I knew from the outset of my writing that this book would not be a scholarly monograph. Instead, I sought to give a window into my life as a newly diagnosed cancer patient as a step along a larger path of faith seeking understanding, a disciple joining with others to follow Jesus Christ. I do develop a set of biblical and theological arguments related to praying the Psalms, providence, and life in Christ as chapter builds on chapter in the book. But I do so in a way that relates my cancer story to the story of God's promise and ongoing action in Christ, by the Spirit. For scholars, students, and pastors, the endnotes might be helpful in hinting at some of the larger academic issues that I have had in mind while writing this book.[2] But they are just hints.

Rather than writing just for an academic audience, I have sought to embrace a genre in this book that can speak to a broad range of Christians—including caretakers, counselors, and those experiencing cancer or some other loss themselves. The genre is not "easy reading," for honestly bringing our laments as mortals before the face of God is never "easy." Nevertheless, I have sought to make the book broadly accessible to inquiring Christians who struggle with questions about how the Triune God's story in Scripture could possibly relate to their calamities of cancer or other trials that seem to leave us in a fog, in lament, and in confusion about God's deliverance.

JTB
Holland, Michigan
January 2015

Acknowledgments

The first and last word of the Christian life is one of gratitude. With regard to this book, I am grateful above all to our covenant Lord and his unrelenting love made known in Jesus Christ. This love is strong and steady and redemptive as we come before the throne of grace with our toughest questions, laments, confusion, and tears.

I am also grateful to God for the gifts of many scholars, pastors, and laypeople who have read portions of the book and have contributed to its refinement. I am responsible for the book's final form, with all of its limitations, but I have received helpful input from several reading groups and individuals who read various parts of the manuscript at various stages. Special thanks go to Michael Allen, Khaled Anatolios, Carol Bechtel, Randy Blacketer, Jim Brownson, Ann Conklin, Robert Cosgrove, Chuck DeGroat, Michael Horton, Kelly Kapic, Brian Keepers, Dustyn Keepers, Matthew Levering, Rob Lister, Andrew McCoy, Suzanne McDonald, Brandon and Stephanie Smith, and Thomas Weinandy. Special thanks to the exceptionally hard work of research assistants who worked on this book at various stages of the process: Alberto LaRosa, Molly Mead, Stephen Shaffer, Kevin Slusher, and Brad Zwiers. Thanks also to Bob Hosack and the whole team at Brazos who have been enthusiastic supporters through the whole process of this book project.

In addition to those who helped directly with the manuscript, I am grateful for many—near and far—who have prayed and supported my family and me in so many ways since my cancer diagnosis. Thank you. I am especially grateful for the support of the community of Western Theological Seminary and my fellow members at First Reformed Church in Holland.

In gratitude, I offer this book as a gift to the church—may God use it for his glory.

Abbreviations

CTS   John Calvin, *Calvin's Commentaries*, trans. Calvin Translation Society, ed. John King, 22 vols. (1845–56; repr., Grand Rapids: Baker, 1981)

Inst.   John Calvin, *Institutes of the Christian Religion, 1559*, ed. J. T. McNeill, trans. F. L. Battles, 2 vols. (Philadelphia: Westminster, 1967)

LW   Martin Luther, *Luther's Works*, ed. Jaroslav Pelikan and Helmut T. Lehmann, vols. 1–30 (St. Louis: Concordia, 1955–86); vols. 31–55 (Philadelphia: Fortress, 1955–86)

OF   *Our Faith: Ecumenical Creeds, Reformed Confessions, and Other Resources* (Grand Rapids: Faith Alive, 2013)

Some sections of this book were originally written on CarePages.com; they have undergone some minor editing, and they are marked in the book as CarePages postings.

1

Walking in the Fog

A Narrowed Future or a Spacious Place?

"Get well soon! Jesus loves you! God is bigger than cancer!"

My tears started to flow as I read these words. They were from a fifteen-year-old girl with Down syndrome in my congregation. Less than a week earlier, the doctor spoke the diagnosis to me, about which he had no doubt: a cancer of the bone marrow, multiple myeloma—an incurable cancer, a fatal disease. I had been in a fog ever since. How was I to face each day when my future—which had seemed wide open—had suddenly narrowed? My "world" seemed to be caving in on itself with fog in each direction I turned, so that no light could shine in.

While I had received many cards in the previous days, this one was different. "God is bigger than cancer!" Yes. She did not say, "God will cure you of this cancer," or "God will suffer with you." God is *bigger* than cancer. The fog is thick, but God is bigger. My cancer story was already developing its own sense of drama. The sky was closing in, enveloping my whole world so that nothing else could creep in. But God's story, the drama of God's action in the world, was bigger. The girl in my church wasn't denying the fog or the loss but testifying to a God who was greater, the God made known in Jesus Christ, who shows us that

1

"the light shines in the darkness, and the darkness did not overcome it" (John 1:5). In my tears, there was not only grief but also joy that in the body of Christ theological truths are not a commodity trafficked and controlled by professional theologians. God's story in Christ is bigger than my cancer story, period.

This book explores the way in which God, and the drama of his revelation in Christ, is bigger than my cancer story. The first six chapters build on one another in their reflection on God's story in relation to my cancer story. They do not give a sequential, month-by-month account, but offer different angles of vision into the reality of diagnosis and my first six months of chemotherapy. In chapters 7 and 8, I continue the story of my cancer chronologically with my theological reflections during nearly a month in the hospital receiving a stem cell transplant. The final two chapters complete my theological reflections on God's story as I emerged from the transplant into a time of quarantine (because of a compromised immune system) and eventually returned to my "old" life, in a new way. This first chapter begins my telling of the cancer story and provides some initial biblical and theological reflections that will be explored further as the book moves into later chapters: how God's story relates to my cancer story; the Psalms as companions in our Christian pilgrimage; the meaning of life in Christ and God's final victory over death.

Living in the Fog: Sharing the Cancer Story and Moving into God's Story

God is bigger than cancer. Yet, from those early days in the fall of 2012, I sensed that my unfolding cancer story was not to be denied or repressed because of God's story, either. The news felt like a heavy burden. When I would see students and colleagues at the seminary where I work (Western Theological Seminary) and respond to their queries of "How are you?," any response I gave felt like a lie. My wife and I decided to share the news publicly—with no "secrets"—within two days of receiving the diagnosis. An emergency faculty meeting was called. No dry eyes. An announcement went out to the seminary community, the church, and friends on Facebook. For better or worse, my cancer journey was no longer just my own or that of my family. It was shared with our community.

There are risks with that kind of sharing, as cancer patients know. Our culture often suggests that we are "entitled" to a long, fulfilling life, and if that doesn't happen, there must be someone to sue, someone to blame. When the word "cancer" is spoken, looking to the future reveals only a fog of uncertainty. It brings to mind a life that is spent in the process of dying—a casket waiting to be filled, with no politician to blame for it. In this state of affairs, people often don't know how to respond. Many simply said that I would be in their prayers. Some shared a Bible verse in encouragement. Some allowed the conversational habit of "free association" to hold sway, sharing about the last person they knew who died of cancer or of someone they knew who had a remarkable recovery from cancer. For the patient, the last approach tends to be the least helpful. And the more public the news is, the more frequently one will hear stories of others with the same cancer who died an early death, herbal remedies that one *must* try, or other less-than-helpful bits of advice.

Whether or not cancer patients intend to share their journey openly with others, they generally find that the cancer situation itself has put their lives into a fish bowl—for public viewing—whether they like it or not. "What were your most recent test results?" "What did the doctor say?" Those questions used to be for me and my family. Now, with a "terminal illness," they are relevant questions for all who care about my family and me. My body—its test results, its symptoms—has become a public spectacle, something for public commentary. Some things are kept private. But much that was formerly private is no longer so.

Sharing the cancer story, however, can also open the door for many blessings to flow. One blessing is that I have been able to explore—and bear witness to—the ways in which God's story intersects with the cancer story; how my cancer story is complicated and mysterious but not nearly as compelling as the mystery of God's love made known in Jesus Christ. This opportunity came with the initial announcement of my diagnosis, where—in all of the various venues—I included the

following words from Question and Answer 1 of the Heidelberg Catechism: "What is your only comfort in life and in death? That I am not
my own, but that I belong—in body and soul, in life and in death—to
my faithful Savior Jesus Christ."[1] Like the note from the fifteen-year-old
girl in my church, it breaks through the fog of "terminal" and "incurable" and "cancer" by pointing us to the bedrock of what matters: that
I belong, in life and in death, to Jesus Christ. My life is not my own.

This opportunity was soon amplified when I began to chronicle both
stories on CarePages, a blog site for those who want to update family
and friends as they struggle with illness. Within a week of my diagnosis, I started chemotherapy. There was a lot of medical information to
be shared. The sharing of that information on an individual basis was
laborious and intense. And overwhelming. I soon decided that starting
a CarePages blog would be wise—to share the medical information
to all who were interested, all who were praying. Moreover, it could
be a forum for sharing the intersection of the two stories that I found
myself in. In many ways, this book is an extension of that initial effort
at sharing, exploring, and testifying to the way in which the drama of
the Triune God intersects with my story of pain and disorientation
due to cancer.

A Narrowed Future, a Spacious Place

Here is a section from my CarePages posted on October 11, 2012,
which was about two weeks after the diagnosis. It gives a taste of the
genuine lament and yet hope in and through Christ that later chapters
will continue to explore.

Psalm 31:7–8:

"I will be glad and rejoice in your love, for you saw my affliction and
knew the anguish of my soul. You have not given me into the hands
of the enemy but have set my feet in a spacious place." (NIV)

One thing about the experience of being diagnosed with cancer is that it feels like a narrowing, a tightening, rather than "a spacious place" to dwell. We all know, in theory, that we are mortal, but in day-to-day life many of us don't live with the thought. As a father of a one- and three-year-old, I tended to think of the next few decades as an open expanse, assuming I would see Neti and Nathaniel grow and mature, graduate from high school, etc. And this may be the case, God willing—I am certainly not giving up hope for those things.

But in being diagnosed with a disease that makes the prospect of life in the coming decades more uncertain, there is a narrowing that takes place. It feels a bit like the lights in distant rooms are turning off or, rather, flickering. They were rooms that you were just assuming would be there for you to pass through in future years. The space starts to feel more constricted, narrowed.

Now, not all of this narrowing is bad. Some things that are, in the big picture of things, unimportant have not merited a second thought since the diagnosis. Other parts of my life, such as faith, family, friends, and vocation, are very significant. The "narrowing" can be a place where we prioritize what is most important. But even as we do so, it can still feel like a small, diminishing place that we occupy.

In light of all of this, it is important to remember a distinctive entryway that Christians have into this Psalm—that through God's victory, our feet have been placed in "a spacious place." Ultimately, to be and to dwell in Christ is to dwell in the most "spacious place" imaginable. In our culture, to focus one's trust and affection on one hope—Jesus Christ—strikes many as narrow or risky. But because of who Jesus Christ is, to dwell in him is to occupy a wide, expansive place. In Revelation 21:6, the risen Christ declares, "I am the Alpha and the Omega, the beginning and the end. To the thirsty I will give water as a gift from the spring of the water of life." Colossians 1:16–17 declares that "in him all things in heaven and on earth were created, things visible and invisible, whether thrones or dominions or rulers or powers—all things have been created through him and for him. He himself is before all things, and in him all things hold together." What could be more wide and capacious than this—to dwell in Christ, the Alpha and Omega, the one through whom all things were made, and in whom all things hold together? What could be more broad and expansive than to share in his life by the Holy Spirit? What could be more spacious than that? In Christ, God has truly given us a "spacious place" to dwell that overcomes death and sin, so we have good reason to "be glad and rejoice" in the love of the Lord.

In the months following, I would return to these themes again and again: a genuine lament and a genuine rejoicing in God's promises—promises that, as expressed in the Psalms, are the basis for praise, trust, and also complaint and lament; promises that find their fulfillment in Jesus Christ, and life in him by the Spirit. But this life in Christ, while abundant, cannot be measured by a life span.

A Shortened Life Span? The Ways of Cancer and of God

A week after the post above, I continued my CarePages reflections after attending a conference in Detroit focused on my cancer, multiple myeloma. The conference raised medical and theological questions: What will this cancer mean for how I view the future? Does God owe me a long life? What would it mean to say that abundant life in Christ cannot be constricted by the length of a life span?

We had a good weekend in Detroit at the conference. "Good." Well, maybe not the best descriptor, but the time together over the weekend was enjoyable and filled with grace, and the conference was very informative. It included presentations on prognosis, chemo and side effects, stem cell transplant, treatment after the disease returns after remission, and so on. It was encouraging at points and

6

sobering at points. Sometimes it was encouraging and sobering at the same moment.

Just to give a snapshot of how it could be both, at one point a presenter spoke about the many new treatments that have come out for multiple myeloma in the last fifteen years, and then cited that the median life span after diagnosis has doubled in the last ten years. Doubled. That's good! The group broke into applause. But it is all a matter of perception. If I would have walked in the room two months ago (before any bad signs from my blood tests) and would have been told that the [new] median life span applied to my condition, I would have been extremely distressed. But nevertheless I do thank God for the many cancer researchers who have been making genuine progress with this disease, and there are encouraging signs, with many drugs in clinical trials right now.

In terms of how many years of life one has after diagnosis, that is something that patients generally want to know, but doctors are much more cautious about estimating with multiple myeloma. For me, I could look at the overall "median" life span, but that could be misleading, as I'd have to keep in mind that the "median" diagnosis age is between sixty-five and seventy, and I am thirty-nine. There are a few tests that can be done to find out a bit more about how aggressive the particular disease is (because that varies from patient to patient). We will ask about those. But all of this information and speculation takes place under the overall, flashing red sign that says "We don't know!" about how long a multiple myeloma patient (or anyone else!) will live.

This place of not knowing is one that sometimes feels like a thick fog for me right now. I could have five years, ten years, or decades. Who knows? Not me. We belong to God—the Alpha and the Omega, who holds time in his hands—but we are not God. We are mortal, and we don't know when we will die. There is a fog for all of us, whether we realize it or not, that as creatures we do not live in the world as individuals who own it but as temporary stewards of God's good gifts.

Right now, I am a steward of God's wonderful gifts of being a spouse to Rachel, a father of Neti and Nathaniel; the lovely, centering gift of friends and other family; the incredible privilege of work and vocation in training seminarians and writing for the church and the academy. Each day comes to us from the gracious hand of God—it is a gift, whether it is our last or one of many more years.

But living into the reality that each day is a gift also involves coming to recognize a stark, biblical truth that is deeply countercultural: that God is not our debtor. God's reply to Job's attempt to make his case before God displays this. "Where were you when I laid the foundation of the earth? Tell me, if you have understanding. Who determined its measurements—surely you know!" (Job 38:4–5). God is God and we are not. The penitent Job responds not by repenting for his lament (for God's people can and should lament) but by a recognition that God is God, and God is not our debtor. "I am unworthy—how can I reply to you? I put my hand over my mouth. I spoke once, but I have no answer—twice, but I will say no more" (Job 40:4–5 NIV).

Surely God is not capricious or untrustworthy. God has disclosed himself as gracious in his dealings with creation, with Israel, and in Jesus Christ. The Triune God binds himself to covenant promises that include, envelop, and hold us in a communion that sin and death cannot break. God is faithful to these promises, fulfilled in Jesus Christ. But this does not mean that things will look "fair" or that we are shielded from all of the present consequences of sin and death. God is not our debtor. He does not "owe" us a certain number of requisite years of life; Christ promises us that he will not leave us orphaned (John 14:18) but not that each of us will live the American dream, comfortably retire, and soak in all of what we think of as "normal" life stages. Each day is a gift. Each year is a gift. Each decade, for each of us, is a gift that comes gratuitously from God's hand, not from our entitlement to live a "normal" life or life span. The "abundant life" that Christ brings (John 10:10) is not measured or contained by years or a life span.

This CarePages entry represents a kind of "first brush" with the existential and theological issues raised by the mixed blessing of a medical prognosis. In the prognosis process, it's hard not to be paralyzed by numbers. About fifteen years ago, the median life span for someone diagnosed with multiple myeloma was two to three years. Now, it is about double that. But what numbers apply to me, as an unusually young patient? It's really hard to tell. One doctor examined my medical results and sought to encourage me by suggesting that I had a good possibility of living longer than some other patients—I had a 50 percent chance of living ten years, he said. What does that mean? I'm either alive or dead. I can't be 50 percent alive, just as a woman cannot be 50 percent pregnant. How am I to think about or process such a number? (Later, another doctor thought that number was too pessimistic for my prognosis.)

My main oncologist tended to leave it more open ended. He would say, "Some patients live decades with multiple myeloma." No promises. But a possible hope. And my life span prospects depend, in his view, largely on the ongoing progress in research and treatment.

In seeking to find out more about the world of cancer, I read the Pulitzer Prize–winning book *The Emperor of All Maladies* by Siddhartha Mukherjee in the months following diagnosis. I found his assessment of multiple myeloma to be quite balanced and illuminating. On the one hand, "in the 1980s, multiple myeloma was treated by high doses of standard chemotherapy—old, hard-bitten drugs that typically decimated patients about as quickly as they decimated the cancer."[2] These chemo drugs had not been developed specifically for myeloma, and the expected life spans were short. But improved treatments, through drugs developed specifically for the disease, have made a big difference. While "myeloma is still a fatal disease," the improvements have been substantial: "In 1971, about half of those diagnosed with multiple myeloma died within 24 months of diagnosis; the other half died by the tenth year."[3] Yet "in 2008, about half of all Myeloma patients treated with the shifting armamentarium of new drugs will still be alive at five years. If the survival trends continue, the other half will continue to be alive well beyond ten years."[4]

But what do these numbers mean? Even if I do live decades, the myeloma may still be chopping decades off of the life that I might have had without cancer. Of course, I never knew that I could or would live until my seventies or older; but often such an assumption is simply present in white, middle-class Western culture, and I had soaked it in. I found myself thinking about these numbers when playing with Neti—my beautiful three-year-old daughter adopted from Ethiopia. Would I see her into middle school? If I listen to the 50-percent-for-ten-years estimate, then that means I have a 50 percent chance to see her live to be thirteen. Wow. What would be my "chances" to see her graduate from high school? And what does "chance" have to do with it, anyway? Why, God, oh why, would you allow this for little Neti and her younger brother, Nathaniel? Rachel and I desired and prayed for children—and both Neti and Nathaniel came as incredible gifts, answers to prayer. Why would you take away their dad during their childhoods?

Lament and the Victory of God over Death

While I seek to affirm the biblical truth that God is not my debtor and does not owe me a long life, my sense of lament becomes acute when I consider my young children in particular. My death would not just be a loss for me and for my wife, Rachel. It would be a tremendous loss for my young children.

Scripture does not say God owes us a long life. But paradoxically, this does not mean that we accept suffering and death with a stoic fatalism. Instead, God's people lament. In the Old Testament, not just the prospect of death but a death in the "middle" of one's years is seen as a particular cause for lament. Biblical scholars have long noted that the belief in a resurrection after death—explicit in passages of a late date such as Daniel 12—was gradual in its development in the Old Testament. Yet Jon Levenson has recently argued that passages like Daniel 12 have deep roots and resonance with many other, earlier parts of the Old Testament: for death—particularly premature or early death—is in tension with the fact that "God promises, offers, and prefers life and

10

saves his people from annihilation."[5] Thus, while the psalmist does not assume an afterlife when he says, "The dead do not praise the LORD, nor do any that go down into silence" (115:17), nevertheless an early death is grounds for protest and lament: "He [the Lord] has broken my strength in midcourse; he has shortened my days. 'O my God,' I say, 'do not take me away at the midpoint of my life, you whose years endure throughout all generations'" (Ps. 102:23–24). The psalmist adds to this plea by noting that God has many years—implicitly suggesting he could spare some more for his servant. "Long ago you laid the foundation of the earth, and the heavens are the work of your hands. They will perish, but you endure; they will all wear out like a garment. You change them like clothing, and they pass away; but you are the same, and your years have no end" (102:25–27). This is praise to the eternal, but also a lament, from one who faces death "at the midpoint of my life."

One finds a similar lament and protest in the book of Isaiah, when Hezekiah—ill to the point of death—"wept bitterly" (38:3) and lamented to the Lord that "in the middle of my days I must depart" (38:10 ESV). There was an offense, a cause for lament and complaint, in being taken from life in the "middle" of one's days.

In the unfolding of God's revelation through Scripture, death itself comes to be seen as God's enemy—contrary to God's desire and promise of life for his people. In the Old Testament, this is apparent in Daniel 12, in which God's people will be "delivered" when they "awake" from their "sleep in the dust of the earth" (vv. 1–2). In the New Testament, this testimony to God's victory over death is widespread and emphatic in light of Jesus Christ. In his marvelous chapter on the resurrection in 1 Corinthians 15, Paul speaks about how Christ's death and resurrection brings victory over death, for Christ's resurrection is the "first fruits, then at his coming those who belong to Christ" (v. 23). For at "the end," the Triune God's rule over "every authority and power" (v. 24) will be complete. "For he must reign until he has put all his enemies under his feet. The last enemy to be destroyed is death" (vv. 25–26).

Thus, in the testimony of Daniel and the apostle Paul, it is not just "premature death" but death itself—as that which would limit the life

God shares with his people—that will be defeated. It is the final enemy. But in the meantime, here in a land in which war, poverty, cancer, and disease take the lives of mortals like you and me, death is still a present enemy. It doesn't seem to make much sense when it comes. At times, death comes to a child from cancer; at times, death comes to those who seem to be in the wrong place at the wrong time, as with those who perished from the Boston Marathon bombing (April 2013); at times, death comes to a ninety-five-year-old whose spouse has passed on after struggling with illness for years. In this final case, for the family, it may feel like death itself is a kind of grace—after a long life, when each breath becomes a burden, a struggle. But still, even then, death is an enemy. It must be overcome if we are to experience the life with God that God himself desires for his people. As John's vision of the heavenly Jerusalem indicates, God's repeated promise that "I will be their God and they will be my people" needs to overcome death in order to have its ultimate fulfillment. For then "He will dwell with them; they will be his peoples, and God himself will be with them" (Rev. 21:3). For "to the thirsty I will give water as a gift from the spring of the water of life" (v. 6).

Embracing the Psalms as Companions for the Journey

God has not promised to spare us from earthly death. But he has conquered it in Christ—death does not have the power to separate us from his love. In the meantime, death's power and its limited reign are causes for lament, for complaint, for protest to the God of life. I don't know whether we will sing psalms of lament in the new Jerusalem, but until that day, the book of Psalms—with its praise, petition, and lament—will continue to be the prayer book of God's people. As I hope to show in various chapters in this book, the Psalms themselves need to be our companions in our current sojourn to the heavenly city. And there are more psalms of lament than any other genre of psalm.[6] We cannot leave them behind.

In taking this approach, I will not try to read the Psalms apart from the rest of the biblical canon or apart from Christ. Together with the

New Testament writers and Christians since the early church, I see God's promises in the Psalms as fulfilled in Jesus Christ. On the other hand, I will not approach the Psalms as simply treatises on Christian doctrine or anticipations of abstract teachings that we receive more clearly in the New Testament. No. The Psalms are God's Word to us—a place God has given us to dwell, to pray, to live; they are given for our healing, our growth into our identity as God's people. Ultimately, like all of Scripture, the Psalms present to us the Word of the Spirit that conforms us into the image of Christ so that we may find our place as adopted sons and daughters of the Father, serving God and neighbor as God's children.

From the early centuries of the church, the Psalms were memorized and used regularly in Christian worship.[7] Fourth-century bishop Athanasius spoke eloquently about how they are God's medicine for humans in all different circumstances: "Whatever your particular need or trouble, from this same book you can select a form of words to fit it, so that you not merely hear and pass on, but learn the way to remedy your ill."[8] Whether in St. Benedict's monasteries or John Calvin's Geneva, a wide range of Christians have experienced the Psalms—in good times and bad—through meditating, praying, and singing. They are ideal for corporate worship as well as personal devotion. And after my diagnosis in September 2012, they took on an especially important role.

In a CarePages entry on October 28, 2012, I wrote,

The Psalms have been my daily companion for years, but since the diagnosis, they have taken on special power. They give moments of orientation—to the promises of our Great God, our rock and our fortress. And they also cry out to God in disorientation—in pain, in confusion, in distress—as well as in joy. The cancer journey so far has already had a lot of ups and downs. And the Psalms are meeting me in those different places—or rather, God is meeting me through the Psalms.

John Calvin has a wonderful way of expressing this: he calls the Psalms "an anatomy of all the parts of the soul." In his preface to his Psalms commentary, he says, "There is not an emotion of which any one can be conscious that is not here represented as in a mirror. Or rather, the Holy Spirit has here drawn to the life all the griefs, sorrows, fears, doubts, hopes, cares, perplexities, in short, all the distracting emotions with which the minds of men are wont to be agitated."[9] All of this is brought before the face of God—all of our fear, anger, joy, and wonder. In a way similar to the point of my first posting about being seen by God, praying the Psalms allows every part of us to come before the Triune God, to be seen by him as his adopted son or daughter—to praise, complain, and even vent before the Almighty. God can handle our laments and our petitions. Our laments pivot on God's promises.

In the last few weeks, my most acute laments have come in thinking and praying about Neti and Nathaniel. Some of it relates to the near future—thinking about how they will respond if the chemo works, and I then go to the hospital for the transplant. Some of the laments relate to the longer-term future, and they're too young to comprehend how what is happening now may relate to that. My kids are such precious gifts. I can't put into words my gratitude to God for them, my love for them. So lamenting for them, for their sake, comes pretty naturally as I sit with the psalmist.

But I also rejoice with the psalmist in God's mighty and faithful acts and promises. . . .

> O give thanks to the LORD, for he is good; for his stead-
> fast love endures forever. (Ps. 107:1)

Praying the Psalms in Christ

Whether you are in a season of rejoicing or lament, praying all of the Psalms should be the practice of Christ followers everywhere. For through the Psalms, God shows us how to pray. God uses the words of the Psalms to reshape our desires and affections. God meets us in the midst of our prayer with and through the Psalms. And we do not pray the Psalms alone. As Dietrich Bonhoeffer points out, it is "David" and others in Israel who pray the Psalms; it is also "the church" that prays the Psalms; and it is also "I myself" who prays the Psalms. But this is made possible because *Jesus Christ* prayed and prays the Psalms. Because Jesus Christ prays the Psalms, those who belong to him (the church as God's people and as individuals) can pray insofar as he or she "participates in Christ."[10] In the words of Bonhoeffer,

> How is it possible for a man and Jesus Christ to pray the Psalter together? It is the incarnate Son of God, who has borne every human weakness in his own flesh, who here pours out the heart of all humanity before God and who stands in our place and prays for us. He has known torment and pain, guilt and death more deeply than we. Therefore it is the prayer of our human nature assumed by him which comes here before God. It is really our prayer, but since he knows us better than we know ourselves and since he himself was true man for our sakes, it is also really his prayer, and it can become our prayer only because it was his prayer.[11]

In and through and by Jesus Christ, with whom Christians have been united by the Holy Spirit, we can praise, lament, petition, and discover that the story of our loss is not the only, or most important, story that encloses our lives. We discover that this spacious place—of living in Christ—is wide and deep enough for us to petition, rejoice, and also join our laments to those of Jesus Christ, who intercedes on our behalf (see Rom. 8:24). Jesus is no stranger to lament. Indeed, Jesus teaches, "Blessed are those who mourn, for they will be comforted" (Matt. 5:4); Jesus laments over the death of Lazarus (John 20:11); he weeps over the unbelief of Jerusalem (Luke 19:41–44); in the garden of Gethsemane, Jesus was "deeply grieved, even to death," and cries out in lament and petition to the Father (Mark 14:34; see also Matt. 26:36–46; Luke 22:39–46); and Jesus cries out with the psalmist on the cross, "My God, my God, why have you forsaken me?" (Ps. 22:1; see also Matt. 27:46; Mark 15:34). In later chapters, we will further explore what it means to join the psalmist in lament and praise as one is united to the Lord Jesus Christ in his death and resurrection. Our lives are not our own, and our stories have been incorporated into the great drama of God's gracious work in the world in Jesus Christ through the Spirit. As we come to sense our role in this drama, we find that it is a path of lament and rejoicing, protest and praise, rooted in trust in the Triune God, the central actor; we can walk on this path even while the fog is thick. For God is bigger than cancer. God is bigger than death. The God of Jesus Christ is the God of life, whose loving promises will be shown as true in the end. Until that time, we wait with the psalmist for the Lord and hope in his Word.

> I wait for the LORD, my soul waits,
>   and in his word I hope;
> my soul waits for the Lord
>   more than those who watch for the morning,
>   more than those who watch for the morning. (Ps. 130:5–6)

2

Sorting through the Questions

The Book of Job, the Problem of Evil, and the Limits of Human Wisdom

Walking into the patient room, my oncologist looked to see that Rachel and I were sitting on the far side of the room, playing tic-tac-toe on a sheet of paper. We smiled and said it wasn't a very good game, but we were very nervous—we needed a way to pass the time. The oncologist laughed and said that it's not easy to have a competitive game of tic-tac-toe among adults. And then his face changed.

Earlier, when Rachel and I met with the oncologist after my initial testing, we were told that my diagnosis was likely to be one of three possibilities: (1) a precancerous condition that would give me a predisposition toward multiple myeloma; (2) a "smoldering" myeloma, which is not an active form of the cancer but becomes active in half of patients within five years; (3) an active form of multiple myeloma. We thought that possibility 1 or 2 was most likely. I am about thirty years younger than the median diagnosis age for myeloma, and I didn't seem to have a lot of symptoms that would indicate number 3. Yet there had been many nights with fitful sleep while awaiting the results of my bone marrow biopsy. There were times of lament—of crying out, "Why God?" For in reality, all three possibilities were bad news. I even speculated that if it was possibility number 3, I'd better draw up a "bucket list"—a trip to Seattle where Rachel and I had taken our honeymoon, a trip to the Boston area, where we still had friends from our time there in graduate school at Harvard.

I had played and replayed the scene in my head so many times that now this moment in the patient room with the oncologist seemed like a dream. In my imagination, it was just one of many times that I was being given a diagnosis. But this time it was for real. The oncologist said the words "active myeloma" (possibility number 3), and Rachel squeezed my hand. Then he told us of the damage it had already done: bone damage to my skull, arm, and hip, and plasma levels over five times of what they should be in my bones. Then he talked about various approaches to "staging"—according to one system, I was stage 1 out of 3; according to another, I was worse. (About a month later I found that I was stage 3 out of 3 according to that staging system.) And then, "You need to start chemotherapy next week." He started to detail some of the challenges in getting insurance approval for these toxic therapies, and the details were lost on me. The meeting seemed unreal—too much to process.

I was expecting bad news. Rachel and I had already spent several weeks talking, lamenting, and processing the news about the three possibilities. But I wasn't expecting it to be this bad. Active myeloma? Chemo next week? The last time I had met with the oncologist, hearing the news about the three possible outcomes, I had a prayer group meeting the same night. That was a gift. When I shared those possibilities, there was an uncomfortable silence. They reflected back to me the gravity of the situation, which I was having a hard time processing. But they also committed the news to prayer. Now, I would need to tell them about this news—not the answer to prayer that they were wanting. And I would need to tell others—there was no turning back at this point. "There is no doubt about this diagnosis," the oncologist said. I needed words to pray—I needed a language for my life with God in this moment.

Lamenting in Grief, Lamenting in Protest

Lament. The English word has some ambiguity, particularly as it relates to the laments in Scripture. It can mean grieving and mourning, such as those weeping for a lost loved one at a funeral; or it can mean protest, a form of petition—seeking to take God to "court" to make one's case. Both senses of "lament" are important in the Bible, and although they differ, there is also a continuum between the two.

Writers of laments and complaints in the Psalms often seek to make their "case" against God, frequently citing God's promises in order to complain that God seems to be forgetting his promises. They throw the promises of God back at him.

> I say to God, my rock,
>   "Why have you forgotten me?
> Why must I walk about mournfully
>   because the enemy oppresses me?"
> As with a deadly wound in my body,
>   my adversaries taunt me,
> while they say to me continually,
>   "Where is your God?" (Ps. 42:9–10)

God is the rock and refuge to his people, the One who always re-members Israel. Based on this promise, the psalmist thrusts the promise back to God in protest: "Why have you forgotten me?" Why does God allow the psalmist's enemies to mock God's promises, tauntingly say-ing, "Where is your God?"

When I shared the news of my cancer diagnosis, the response of my friends and family was varied. Sometimes it was lament, in the sense of mourning and grieving. There were many tears. Sometimes those responding quickly moved to remind me of God's promises and of their commitment to pray for me and my family. And, less often, there were responses in the mode of protest-lament, as in this note from a friend (used with permission).

Thanks so much for taking the time to talk tonight. . . .

19

I wanted to apologize because what I wanted to say didn't manage to come out. It's beautiful just how much better the little girl from your church was able to articulate it. God is bigger than cancer. It's true. And also, perhaps less faithfully . . . I hate this for you more than anything. I hate this for your family. I want you to beat the heck out of it.

Forgive us all for the stupid things we say and don't say. I am praying tonight for you and Rachel.

I remember the moment when I received this note. I didn't feel the anger that she felt. I had to command all of my energy in order to face the new regimen of chemotherapy and the immediate changes that my family was facing. I didn't feel like I had the energy to be angry, to complain in protest to God. But this note stuck in my mind. I was grateful for it immediately because it felt like a gift from another member of the body of Christ—they can be angry on my behalf. This anger is not "less faithful"; it is faithful in bringing a suit before God on my behalf, even when I am far too tired and preoccupied to do so myself. And months later, at times when my grief turned a corner toward a plea of "Why, God?," her earlier angry, grieving prayer was a kind of solace.

When Tragedy Hits: The Sufferer's Questions

What questions are pressing for those who are in crisis, whose world has been deeply shaken? Pastoral counselors often take a guess at what those in crisis are experiencing: some assume that they are most likely to be asking deep, existential questions about the problem of evil— "How could this happen, God?" Other pastors may assume that if the sufferer offers an expression of praise or trust, it must be a disingenuous conformity to an overly cheery Christian community. At other times, pastors assume that those in crisis won't be asking any *real* theological questions but are just entering into the well-mapped process of grief and grieving. Still others may assume that the solace that is needed can be (quickly) provided by a felicitously chosen Bible verse.

20

In the wake of my own diagnosis and entrance into chemo, I can say that my response was not simple. At times I would cry out in grief to God; along with this, I would lament in protest to God for the sake of my young children. At times I responded in gratitude for—and awe of—all of the gifts that God had already given, even if my life were not to be extended much longer. God is faithful to his promises, and his loving gifts each day are lavish and amazing—and I sometimes sensed that deeply. I found myself taking solace in these different yet complementary modes of praying and living before God: lament in grieving, praise, lament in protest, trust. There were many open questions—more than I could embody or express at any given moment. Thus, the diversity of modes of praying that I found in the Psalms—and in the Christian community around me—was a buoy. When people asked, "How are you doing?," any response I gave was just the tip of the iceberg. At any given moment, I wasn't a very competent expert on how I was. But to get in touch with the rest of the iceberg, I didn't need to look further than to the modes of prayers, questions, and convictions in the book of Psalms.

What about the (allegedly) common question for sufferers—the problem of evil? Did I find myself demanding a rational answer to the question of how an almighty and benevolent God could allow this to happen to me? After the diagnosis a family member gave me a book called *God and Cancer*, where the author discusses several non-Christian religious perspectives on the problem of evil and then claims that "biblical Christianity" provides "the only solution to the problem of evil."[1] I respectfully disagree. Although I had live questions that *related* to the problem of evil, in my view the biblical "answer" to the speculative problem of evil is this (drum roll, please): we don't have an answer. It's not that the Bible hasn't addressed the question so that we as humans are left with a shoulder-shrugging "I don't know." The Bible *has* addressed the question, and God's response—as in the book of Job—is that humans don't have an answer to the problem of evil, and we shouldn't claim that we have one. It should remain an open question, one that we continue to ask in prayer and in our lives in response to the world's suffering. I believe that in Christ God *is* renewing the

21

whole of creation from the alienation, suffering, and evil that corrupts it. But the speculative theodicy question—of "why" our loving and powerful God has permitted tragedy—is ultimately "unanswerable in this life" for "only God can answer, and God has not answered (yet)."[2] The book of Job certainly gives examples of *wrong* human answers to the problem of evil and suffering. But more than that, it insists that answering the theoretical problem of evil is actually beyond the limits of human wisdom.[3]

Sorting through the Questions with the Book of Job

Job is a powerful book that pushes us to reframe our urgent questions—identifying which questions are dead ends and which ones we should keep asking. Reading Job as part of the biblical canon along with the book of Psalms, there is no doubt that we ought to bring both praise and protest, trust and grief, before our God. Job brings all of these before God—including his raw grief and protest in the face of suffering. He laments in grief and protest against God. Later in the book, God testifies that it is Job who has "spoken of me what is right" rather than his friends who refrain from lament (Job 42:7). In the end, after presenting his case to God that the Almighty has been unjust, Job hears God's response and is brought to the point of recanting his case. But Job does not confess lament as a sin against God, for it is not. Rather he comes to recognize the limits of human wisdom before the awesome face of the sovereign Lord: "I recant and relent, being but dust and ashes" (Job 42:6 NJPS).[4] In his relenting, Job "admits that his own wisdom is limited; he bows to a God whose wisdom is limitless."[5]

While endorsing the combination of praise and lament in prayerful living before God, the Job narrative cuts through theoretical attempts to "answer the problem of evil" or give a "theodicy" that claims to know God's reason for allowing evil. Job "was blameless and upright, one who feared God and turned away from evil" (Job 1:1). Yet great evil befell him—his hard-earned fortune was lost, his children suddenly killed, his body covered with painful sores (Job 1–2). To some readers it may feel like a setup for a modern theodicy: Why have bad things happened to a good person like Job? Perhaps the book of Job gives us the answer.

But as one continues in the narrative of Job, this question is not answered; in fact, the theodicy question is shown to be a red herring, a question that "Job's hapless counselors get lost following" but that the narrative itself displaces.[6] The structure of the narrative adds to our expectations that we will discover the divine secret for human suffering: it starts in the heavenly court, where Satan claims that Job's righteous fear of God is simply the result of his happy circumstances. "Does Job fear God for nothing? Have you not put a fence around him and his house and all that he has, on every side? You have blessed the work of his hands, and his possessions have increased in the land. But stretch out your hand now, and touch all that he has, and he will curse you to your face" (1:9–11). The Lord first agrees to allow Satan to have power over Job's family and possessions. When Job still does not curse God, the Lord allows more power to Satan: Job himself "is in your power; only spare his life" (2:6). (Note that in the book of Job, "Satan" [lit. "*the satan*," meaning "the accuser"] is a member of the heavenly court. It is best not to conflate "the satan" in Job with "the devil" in later Jewish and Christian theology.)[7] While it is clear that no affliction can come upon Job apart from the permission of the sovereign Lord, our questions are left unanswered as to why God would allow Job to undergo this suffering.

Job and a Theology of Retribution

While the opening chapters of Job do not answer the question of why God allowed Job to be afflicted, chapters 3–27 of the book are filled with questions—the questions of Job and of Job's friends. Job's friends Eliphaz, Bildad, and Zophar advocate a theology of "retribution": that God rewards the righteous and punishes the wicked. Thus, reasoning in a retroactive and mechanistic way, Job's "friends" think that since this evil has befallen Job, he must be guilty of some sin that he is not disclosing. Job also affirms a theology of retribution through most of the book—with the central difference in Job's response being that he maintains his innocence. Although Job's friends do not know this, the readers know that God himself agrees with Job about his innocence, having testified that Job is "blameless" (1:1, 8; 2:3). In contrast, Job's friends don't know how little they know.

The friends' theology of retribution is not wholly mistaken—the Psalms, Proverbs, and many other parts of Scripture testify to the proverbial truth that they speak. "The wicked will not stand in the judgment, nor sinners in the congregation of the righteous; for the LORD watches over the way of the righteous, but the way of the wicked will perish" (Ps. 1:5–6). The book of Job is not simply a polemic against a theology of "retribution"—arguing that wickedness is *not* punished and righteousness is *not* rewarded. In life and in the testimony of Scripture it is often the case that the way of the wicked brings destruction, while righteousness is rewarded. As Gerald Janzen writes, "If Job's friends were simply and totally wrong—if there is no sense in which justice operates in the world—the only sane response on our part should be to go mad."[8]

Yet for the book of Job as for the ministry of Christ himself, a theology of retribution should not be used as a weapon against sufferers: we should not tell sufferers to look back over their lives in search of a secret sin that is causing their distress. Stated more technically, a theology of retribution should not be used to speculate retroactively about God's reason for allowing suffering. Jesus addressed this directly: "'Rabbi, who sinned, this man or his parents, that he was born blind?' Jesus answered, 'Neither this man nor his parents sinned; he was born blind so that God's works might be revealed in him'" (John 9:2–3). Jesus refuses to grant a mechanistic, retrospective reasoning based in retribution that speculates about why this man was born blind. Was his blindness caused by his sin? No. If we were hoping that Jesus would give us a theodicy, we are sorely disappointed. He affirms that even the blindness will be used by God and goes on to respond to the sufferer, healing him (9:6–7).

Was Job's suffering caused by his sin? The Bible makes the answer clear: no. Thus, although at times suffering *may* come as a result of sin, we cannot judge sufferers based on the fact that they are suffering. It may just be "undeserved" suffering, however "unjust" that is from our human perspective.[9]

I recall how I did my best to search for a "cause" for my multiple myeloma shortly after my diagnosis. Intuitively, it was a pressing question. What did I do to "deserve" this? What was the cancer's cause? There are some cancers (e.g., lung cancer) in which there may be a clearly discernible cause from the action of the patient. But as my oncologist told me in response to my urgent question of causality, "We don't know." We have no idea, really. There is no known cause. From our human standpoint, it just happens. On this particular point, the suffering of Job seems parallel to my own: his suffering was not the result of anything that he did. Sometimes, suffering or calamity is the result of our actions. But Job's was not. And much suffering in the world is not unlike Job's suffering, or my suffering with cancer. Our theodicy question—which demands to know the causal reason for "why"—is left unanswered.

While sometimes a rigid form of retribution theology makes us search for what we did to "deserve" a tragedy (in retrospect), at other times it relates more directly to how Christians view the future. Many Christians don't seem to expect to suffer—assuming that if we are "good Christians" who "obey God's will," then we might face obstacles, but not great tragedies that appear senseless. But in this form as well, the book of Job breaks through our illusions, for it "shatters the myth that our own righteousness can protect us from unjust suffering."[10] God has not given us a bargain such that he would spare us of unjust suffering if we seek to obey his will. To the contrary, in Jesus Christ, we are called to take up our crosses daily and follow the path of the One who was unjustly crucified.

Job's Suit against God, and the Limits of Human Wisdom

Knowing that his suffering was not the result of his own action, Job wants to bring a suit before God: "Oh, that I knew where I might find him, that I might come even to his dwelling! I would lay my case before him, and fill my mouth with arguments. . . . There an upright person could reason with him, and I should be acquitted forever by my judge" (Job 23:3–4, 7). Job's case against God, in fact, is based partly on a theology of retribution: God is not treating him justly because, as a blameless person, Job should be able to expect blessing, not torment. There is a similar sense—of poetic justice violated—behind the demand for the theodicy question to be answered.

Yet what is God's response? Once again, it is a question-reframing response:

> Then the LORD answered Job out of the whirlwind:
>
> "Who is this that darkens counsel by words without knowledge?
> Gird up your loins like a man,
>   I will question you, and you shall declare to me.
>
> "Where were you when I laid the foundation of the earth?
>   Tell me, if you have understanding.
> Who determined its measurements—surely you know!
>   Or who stretched the line upon it?" (Job 38:1–5)

God changes the subject. God gives four chapters of discourse (38–41) that emphasize the utter freedom of God in creating the world and the huge distance between God's viewpoint and human understanding. God doesn't explain why suffering happens to Job or to humans in general. Even by the end of the book of Job, we as readers still don't know.

Yet God's freedom is not capricious—even God's speaking to Job from the whirlwind was a gracious act of mercy. Carol Bechtel compares it to being "a bit like Einstein taking time out to explain the theory of general relativity to his beagle. . . . Einstein knows that the beagle has not got a prayer of understanding the true explanation. So Einstein gives the faithful beagle what he *does* need and *can*, in fact, comprehend: a reality check. 'You are a beagle,' he says with admirable patience. 'I am a brilliant scientist. I love you enough to take time out for this little

26

talk, but you must know you're out of your league.'"[11] If God is truly God and we are not, it is a loving and gracious act of God to tell us that our creaturely wisdom is limited; we can and should lament and respond to evil and suffering in our midst. But only God has a God's-eye perspective that answers why it has been allowed.

God Is God and We Are Not: The Futility of Human "Solutions" to the Problem of Evil

Instead of having his theodicy question answered, Job realizes what it means to be "dust and ashes" (42:6) before the almighty God. It does not mean that we avoid lament. But it *does* mean that our questions are humbled and reframed as we recognize the limits of human wisdom. To say this is not to shut off our minds or settle for a "pat answer." It is a way of admitting that we don't have a human explanation for the problem of evil, for God is God and we are not. Those words are simple enough, but in my own life it has taken a long journey to understand what this biblical truth means.

I remember the surge of energy that came over me when exploring the problem of evil as a student at a Christian college, Wheaton College in Illinois. In high school, I had frequently talked with non-Christian friends and acquaintances about the faith. At times, they would raise "the problem of evil" as an objection. I gave a response about the necessity of God giving human freedom if we were to be able to really love God, but I wasn't completely satisfied with the answer. It wasn't until I experienced the faithful freedom of being able to ask hard questions in a Christian context that I was able to return to the question with vigor.

As I explored the question as a student, I could see that my earlier response about human freedom was a partial explanation, but it didn't fully explain how and why a benevolent, almighty God would allow horrific evil in the world. Perhaps if we emphasize the complete, libertarian freedom of human beings, the problem of evil would be solved? Or, if I was really desperate for a solution, perhaps some form of "universal salvation" would solve the problem?

My encounter with the work of Russian novelist Fyodor Dostoyevsky destroyed the plausibility of these possibilities as "solutions" to the problem of evil. In a memorable conversation in *The Brothers Karamazov*, Ivan Karamazov tells the story of a horrific death of an eight-year-old boy. "The general orders them to undress the boy; the child is stripped naked, he shivers, he's crazy with fear, he doesn't dare make a peep. . . . 'Sic him!' screams the general and looses the whole pack of wolfhounds on him. He hunted him down before his mother's eyes, and the dogs tore the child to pieces."[12] In speaking about this example, Ivan considers the possibility that the oppressors are "repaid" for their evil with hell, or that the child's suffering is somehow made to be "worth it" because of the larger harmony of the world. Ivan, as a skeptic, rejects those possibilities. "But what do I care if they are avenged, what do I care if the tormenters are in hell, what can hell set right here, if these ones have already been tormented? I want to forgive, and I want to embrace, I don't want more suffering. And if the suffering of children goes to make up the sum of suffering needed to buy truth, then I assert beforehand that the whole of truth is not worth such a price."[13] Ivan raises a problem that is not relegated only to Christians who strongly emphasize the sovereignty of God. Giving a libertarian account of human freedom doesn't solve Ivan's problem. Believing hell is empty doesn't solve Ivan's problem either. The problem persists: Why did God allow human freedom at such a price—such that he would allow the horrific suffering of a child? How could a good and almighty God possibly allow senseless suffering and death, as in the death camps of World War II? While I don't share Ivan's skeptical response, I felt the force of it: if freedom costs this much, then it is "too high a price on harmony; we can't afford to pay so much for admission. And therefore I hasten to return my ticket."[14]

To make matters worse, as I read Scripture, many passages did not seem at all concerned to get God "off the hook" for evil. Now don't misunderstand me: I affirm that sin has its origin in human creatures, not in God. But the psalms of lament repeatedly hold God "responsible" for evil in some sense. They wrestle with and even blame God in their crisis—a point that future chapters will examine in detail. In the book of Job, even the accuser, Satan, is not able to act apart from the permission of the sovereign Lord. Indeed, in Isaiah, a consequence of the repeated declaration that "I am the Lord and there is no other" is words that are likely to make us squirm:

> I am the Lord, and there is no other.
> I form light and create darkness,
>   I make weal and create woe;
>   I the Lord do all these things. (Isa. 45:6–7)

While in context I do not think that these words make God the direct author of sin and evil,[15] it is striking how passages such as this—and the book of Job—don't seem to share our contemporary concern to get God completely off the hook for evil. The Lord is almighty, and nothing is outside the realm of his power; the world is in the hands of God. As we will explore in later chapters, that does not mean that God directly and immediately causes everything that happens—there are agents with their own wills who act against God. But we should never confuse our proper affirmation of the freedom and sinfulness of humanity with a complete "explanation" for why there is evil—horrific evil, even directed toward children—in the world.

Responding to Evil as Creatures: Acting as Characters in God's Story, Not as Authors of History

Whether our concern is "Why do I have cancer?" or "Why do children suffer horrifically?" or "How could there be a hell if God is good and almighty?," we are left not with airtight, rational explanations but with Scripture's narrative of a sovereign, loving, and holy God. Our job is not to try to "be God" and rethink how God could have run the universe. Instead, as mortal creatures we should recognize the limits of human wisdom and enter into our humble yet exalted place as sinners who have been reconciled to the Triune God through Jesus Christ. We enter as characters in the middle of the story, not as authors of the story

29

who know all of the reasons God allowed the fall or this evil event. We may have partial explanations—and those partial explanations have usefulness in certain contexts. (For example, it can be appropriate to offer a "defense" of the basic rationality of the Christian faith in light of the problem of evil, as long as one does not claim to know God's reasons for allowing evil. But a defense should be clearly distinguished from a modern "theodicy," which claims to know God's reasons.)[16] Ultimately, we need to admit that we *don't know* God's reasons for permitting evil. It is beyond the realm of human knowledge, and that is part of our creaturely condition.

In light of this response to evil, how might I respond to the objections of Ivan Karamazov? On the one hand, I would agree that I don't know of the reasons that could possibly justify the horrific, unjust death of a child. We should not pretend that we are the authors of history who can say what reasons could possibly justify this. We don't know. But there is one thing that Christians know without a doubt: that suffering and evil require our compassionate response. The present world of suffering is not the way that things are supposed to be. Such unjust suffering is a scandal, and we should cry out to God in our hearts and with our compassionate action.

This response to Ivan's questions does not claim to have a God's-eye view of why there is evil. But it does sustain a proper creaturely response—one that Ivan himself, in his move away from belief in God, was *not* able to maintain. As Ivan himself says later in the novel, "Without God and the future life? It means everything is permitted now, one can do anything? 'Didn't you know?'"[17] Albert Camus observes, "The same man [Ivan] who so violently took the part of innocence, who trembled at the suffering of a child, from the moment that he rejects divine coherence and tries to discover his own rule of life, recognizes the legitimacy of murder. If all is permitted, he can kill his father or at least allow him to be killed."[18] Without belief in a God of justice (to whom he could complain and protest), Ivan actually loses his grounds for acting against injustice in the world; in doing so, Ivan becomes complicit in profound injustice himself.

Asking with Peter, "Lord, to Whom Shall We Go?"

But wouldn't we prefer a different kind of God? Why can't we have a God who answers our questions without reframing and confounding them? If so, then we had better avoid the God of the book of Job and the Psalms, and the God of Jesus Christ. We serve a God who loves us, but loves us freely—and a God who, in Jesus Christ, calls us to costly discipleship. In a CarePages entry, I reflect on this in light of my cancer journey.

I've been thinking a lot about John 6 and Peter's question recently in light of my cancer journey.

"On hearing it, many of his disciples said, 'This is a hard teaching. Who can accept it?'" (John 6:60 NIV). You have to admire the honesty of the disciples. They are right in naming Jesus's teaching as often "hard." They didn't domesticate or rationalize it but named it rightly. In this case, Jesus's teaching was in response to their question of what the work of God requires: "This is the work of God, that you believe in him whom he has sent" (6:29). Easy enough, right? Nope. For Jesus this involves nothing less than finding your treasure in someone other than yourself—dwelling and abiding in Christ, feeding on him as nourishment, as food and drink—thus they should "not work for the food that perishes, but for the food that endures for eternal life, which the Son of Man will give you" (6:27). Wow. It's getting harder and harder. We are to find life in Christ and nourishment in him, not in ourselves and our own resources. That is a hard teaching. And, after hearing this hard teaching, "many of his disciples turned back and no longer followed him" (John 6:66 NIV).

In the last few weeks, though, I've been rediscovering a later verse, which is a climax of sorts for this passage: "Simon Peter answered him, 'Lord, to whom can we go? You have the words of eternal life. We have come to believe and know that you are the Holy One of God'" (6:68–69). Peter's confession is right and beautiful. But don't

31

forget that this question is in light of Jesus's hard teaching about finding nourishment in Jesus Christ rather than their own resources, and "many of his disciples turned back" after his teaching. In light of this, it's the *question* of Peter I keep coming back to. Another way to get at Peter's question would be to put it this way: "Lord, you give us hard teaching, but where else are we supposed to go? We have nowhere else to go, no one else to go to. Looking beyond ourselves and finding our life in you may not sound attractive, but we have nowhere else to go—because you are the One who speaks the words of eternal life, you are Israel's Holy One." As one commentator says about Peter's words here, "There's no one else to go to! They who have (truly) seen and (truly) heard Jesus know that there is none beside him."[19]

When we are in need, like in a cancer journey, we really know how deeply Peter's question strikes. We serve a God who does not promise to be convenient, who does not promise to put our own preferences at the center. Indeed, we serve a God who speaks to us words in Christ such as, "If any want to become my followers, let them deny themselves and take up their cross daily and follow me" (Luke 9:23). In many ways, it would be nicer to have the therapeutic god of American culture who is always tolerant, never requires much of us, and just affirms what we do and provides a pathway to our own happiness. Maybe this would be a God who always cures cancer in exchange for fervent prayer, shows his favor with monetary and physical rewards, or makes a hero of every cancer survivor. Yet even though this kind of therapeutic god is common in American culture, such a god is revealed to be an idol by the One who calls us to deny ourselves and take up our cross, to lose our lives for his sake, to find life—not in ourselves but in nourishment in Christ. Peter's question is an honest one that cuts through our pretenses. It would be nice to serve a master who did not have hard teaching. But really, where else are we to go? When we're in need, we're not just trying to pass a "correct theology" test. We want results. There is an attraction to these idols. But really, where else are we to go? Jesus is the "I am," he is the way, he is the One. Deep down we know that we follow Christ the Lord in our need not because he is the most "convenient" view of God around but because he is the Holy One of God who gives us the words of life. With Peter, we realize that many of the most important things in life are completely and utterly out of our control. So we pray, seek to abide, and seek to obey and "wait on the Lord," as the psalmist frequently says. We have nowhere else to go. Really. We're fooling ourselves unless we admit that: nowhere else to go.

Where else are we to go? Perhaps we could develop some self-soothing scenarios that answer the theodicy question rather than present the open question before God in lament, as Job does. Perhaps we could serve a God who is more tame and docile, who fits our culture's definition of "love" but isn't a holy God who judges sin. Perhaps we could find a God who doesn't say the sorts of hard things that Jesus does. But as Mark Galli says, "The problem with these scenarios is that we know we've made them up to comfort ourselves. . . . When we're alone in the dark, faced with our own mortality, such ideas can be of no comfort because we know where they came from."[20] For true hope in the face of death, we have nowhere else to go besides the Word of God, which finds its fulfillment in Jesus Christ, the "Holy One of God," as Peter testified (John 6:69). In praise and in lament, in life and in death, we hope in this Holy One of God because truly, we have nowhere else to go.

3

Lamenting in Trust

*Praying with the Psalmist amid
a Sea of Emotions*

On the morning after hearing the news that a precancerous malady was likely, with cancer possible, I was downstairs, shedding tears of pain and anxiety. Rachel came downstairs with our seventeen-month-old son, Nathaniel, while our daughter continued to sleep upstairs. At the breakfast table, I told Rachel that after researching online, I found that a precancerous malady would be very likely to eventually move into cancer—whether after five years or ten years. This is not what we wanted for our family. This is not what we wanted for our lives. The fear, the uncertainty, was palpable. As we wept together, Nathaniel started bawling in his high chair as well. He didn't know why Mom and Dad were crying, but he knew that this was not the normal breakfast routine. Rachel and I dried our tears and attempted to console Nathaniel. But his crying continued, big tears rolling down his face.

Several weeks later we received news that rather than a benign yet ominous precancerous malady, my illness was already cancer. Not only that, but the cancer had already been eroding my bones. After receiving this news, my doctor and I could see a likely explanation as to why I had been sick so many times in the last few years: pneumonia, bronchitis, a constant cold, and several other infections. My immune system had been compromised—a common symptom of my cancer. But within a week of this diagnosis, I was to start chemotherapy, which made my previous list of symptoms seem miniscule.

Chemotherapy is poison. Good chemotherapy is poison that is focused quite specifically on a particular cancer rather than a more "general" poison for the body. But many of the medications that I started that week were to counter the side effects of the chemotherapy itself. Overnight, the number of pills I took each day multiplied, and my schedule quickly filled up with visits to the cancer office to receive an IV and chemo shots. I was usually the youngest patient at the cancer office by decades.

There is nothing introspective about physical pain. I recall one procedure, a bone marrow biopsy, where I was lying on my stomach on a paper sheet on top of a treatment table. A large needle was placed into one of the bones in my back. Even though there was a local anesthetic, the pain shot throughout my body's bones like an electric shock. When I sat up, there was blood on the table and on the floor. My friend, who had given me a ride to the cancer center, gave me a forced smile as I stood up. The paper sheet was wet with sweat.

When the pain hit, all I could do was focus my mind in a certain direction. "I can do all things through Christ who strengthens me . . . through Christ who strengthens me, through Christ . . ." Paul's words to the Philippians came to mind (Phil. 4:13) and became my mind's focus point during the pain. It wasn't a meaningless mantra. I needed to be confessing a truth that made such endurance of pain both possible and purposeful—going before God's presence in the raw pain.

At other times during chemo, I struggled with the effects of steroids, which would make my mind race like . . . it was on steroids! For some myeloma patients, the effect was not just an undesired mental alertness but a burst of physical energy: the wife of one patient told me with a smile that she would wake up the morning after her husband had been on steroids, finding that he had been up all night cleaning the house! For me, the steroids caused a flood of mental activity for a few days and then a steep slide into deep fatigue on other days. My dosage varied, but on some days it was ten times the dosage ordinarily prescribed for steroids. The steroids helped to make the chemotherapy more effective without adding further toxins. It was required, not optional.

On many evenings, when I was trying to settle my energetic mind, I lay down on the living room floor and repeated the following words from the opening of Psalm 27.

> The LORD is my light and my salvation—
>> whom shall I fear?
> The LORD is the stronghold of my life—
>> of whom shall I be afraid?
>
> When the wicked advance against me
>> to devour me,
> it is my enemies and my foes
>> who will stumble and fall.
> Though an army besiege me,
>> my heart will not fear;
> though war break out against me,
>> even then I will be confident.
>
> One thing I ask from the LORD,
>> this only do I seek:
> that I may dwell in the house of the LORD
>> all the days of my life,
> to gaze on the beauty of the LORD
>> and to seek him in his temple. (vv. 1–4 NIV)

This prayer was hard work. I had to repeat these words many times for them to become my prayer. Gradually, my mind would focus, tense muscles would release, and I was brought into a place that was not just the story of my cancer, my steroids, my chemo. By the Spirit, I was led into God's presence with my fear, with my anger, and with my hope being recentered on life with God, to "dwell in the house of the LORD all the days of my life, to gaze on the beauty of the LORD and to seek him in his temple." The fight with cancer was not repressed or left behind: "though an army besiege me . . . though war break out against me." But in praying the Psalms—in soaking in its words—I was moved toward trust, and even hope. "My heart will not fear . . . even then I will be confident." In the busyness of day-to-day life, I was not always in touch with my fear, anger, and need for hope during this time on chemo. But praying this psalm both put me in touch with these realities of my life and helped those realities to be reframed as I moved to trust in the Lord and his promises.

Our Hearts Reshaped: Praying Together with the Psalmist

There is nothing automatic about trusting and hoping in God. I don't believe that trusting God is an achievement accomplished through our own efforts—the Spirit alone enables us to confess that Christ is Lord (1 Cor. 12:3), and faith itself is a gift (Eph. 4:7–8). But the Spirit's work in these ways does not *bypass* our own capacities. The Spirit breathes life into them. While God is free to accomplish his purposes by whatever means he chooses, the Spirit graciously comes to the people of God in the midst of their practices of worship centered on God's Word; in corporate worship, with God's Word in proclamation and sacrament; in personal meditation on Scripture; and specifically, in corporate and private praying in and through the Psalms. In the Psalms, we have a prayer book through which God puts us on the path of trusting in his promises.

While the Psalms reflect a very broad range of human emotions, it is not just a human book about human emotions. Praying the Psalms brings our whole heart before the face of God, reorienting our own vision toward God and his promises. As Augustine describes with particular insight, the Psalms are given to us as a divine pedagogy for our affections—God's way of reshaping our desires and perceptions so that they learn to lament in the right things and take joy in the right things.[1]

Specifically, we need to learn how to mourn for that which injures the body of Christ and leads away from Christ's kingdom, and rejoice in the promises of God fulfilled in Christ. The Psalms are given to us by God to guide our prayer and to transform us more and more into our identity in Christ, as members of the body of Christ.

Practicing the Christian faith not only includes beliefs and actions that characterize the community that the Spirit has united together; it also involves displaying the fruit of the Spirit through the reshaping of our hearts so that we respond with delight, grief, anger, and empathy in a way that is fitting for our love of God and neighbor. How do we respond when we read online about a Christian leader who admits a moral failure? What if—horror of horrors—that Christian has different political commitments than us? In viewing the failure of another Christian—particularly one with an ideological difference—we may disorder our affections in response: perhaps we celebrate the event by sharing an article about the scandal on Facebook, along with a condescending comment, delighting in an ideological victory rather than grieving for the sin and the compromise of the church's witness. With the psalmist we could petition for God to "save us, O LORD our God" (106:47) for "we have sinned, even as our ancestors did; we have done wrong and acted wickedly" (106:6 NIV). How do we respond to a member of our congregation who faces crisis? Some of us are quick to offer prayers for an instant fix but less quick to join them with the psalmist in grieving lament before the Lord.

> Be merciful to me, LORD, for I am in distress;
>> my eyes grow weak with sorrow,
>> my soul and body with grief.
> My life is consumed by anguish
>> and my years by groaning;
> my strength fails because of my affliction,
>> and my bones grow weak. (Ps. 31:9–10 NIV)

Others of us offer empathy but do not point the sufferer back to our one hope in God's promise. Yet the biblical laments cry out to

39

the covenant Lord. And as Psalm 62 testifies, "For God alone my soul waits in silence, for my hope is from him. He alone is my rock and my salvation, my fortress; I shall not be shaken." Rather than being one-dimensional, our affections need to become agile and multidimensional through being reshaped by God through the Psalms. Let us grieve and protest and trust and praise together before the Lord. The Psalms give us a way to pray in many keys, major and minor, while directing us to the source of our true hope: the Lord and his promises.

It is not a new idea that the church needs to be shaped by praying the many keys of the Psalms. In the Benedictine cycle of prayer, participants pray through the entire book of Psalms on a weekly basis as a spiritual exercise. In the Reformation, praying the Psalms became the practice in John Calvin's Geneva and scores of other churches in the Reformed tradition. Specifically in Geneva, Psalms would be sung and prayed during three services a week, with the congregation singing thirty stanzas or more weekly at times.[2] In regular corporate worship, psalms of lament and penitence were particularly common, with joyful psalms of praise animating the singing accompanying the Lord's Supper.

A Stinging Loss: Bypassing the Psalms of Lament

In my own experience, full psalms of lament have rarely been used in corporate worship. Lectionaries often delete the raw cries of lament or anger or confusion in the Psalms. And churches that don't follow lectionaries tend to be even more selective—choosing a psalm of thanksgiving from here or there, or choosing verses of trust from psalms of lament while leaving out the complaint itself. Likewise, contemporary hymnals tend to have a far smaller proportion of laments than the book of Psalms does.[3]

Particularly since my diagnosis, I feel this as a stinging loss. While psalms of thanksgiving are wonderful, they are rarer in the book of Psalms than psalms of lament. Cherry-picking only the praises from the Psalms tends to shape a church culture in which only positive

40

emotions can be expressed before God in faith. Since my diagnosis with cancer, I've found that my fellow Christians know how to rejoice about answered prayer and also how to petition God for help, but many don't know what to do when I express sorrow and loss or talk about death. In some sense, this lack of affective agility in their faith is not surprising since our corporate worship has lost many of the elements that are so prominent in the psalms of lament. Somehow, expressions of deep grief and loss have been evacuated from the sanctuary. As Carl Trueman notes,

> The psalms as the staple of Christian worship, with their elements of lament, confusion, and the intrusion of death into life, have been too often replaced not by songs that capture the same sensibilities—as the many great hymns of the past did so well—but by those that assert triumph over death while never really giving death its due. The tomb is certainly empty; but we are not sure why it would ever have been occupied in the first place.[4]

As a result, when we inevitably face the reality of death—along with the fear, anger, and grief faced during other hardships—we are not encouraged to bring those "to church"; such emotions have come to be frowned on as "unreligious." When worship expresses only "victory," it can unintentionally suggest that the broken and the lonely and the hurting have no place here. The message can be, "If you want to fit in, first get your emotions in order so that you can be positive, and then go to worship." But the Psalms help show us that bottling up or trying to "fix" those emotions ourselves is not the right way. In commenting on Psalm 62:8, "pour out your heart before him; God is a refuge for us," Calvin rightly notes that when we face a crisis, "we are all too apt at such times to shut up our affliction in our breast—a circumstance which can only aggravate the trouble and embitter the mind against God." In contrast, a better way is "disburdening our cares to him, and thus, as it were, pouring out our hearts before him."[5] Fear, anger, confusion, protest—these are all emotions that we can and should bring before our covenant Lord with the psalmists.

41

Lamenting before the Face of God: Finding Our Place in the Drama of God

On the one hand, we are to lay open our hearts—with all of their half-formed desires and uncomfortable emotions—before the covenant Lord. Yet on the other hand, the Psalms don't offer us a cheap form of "therapy" that simply expresses emotions for their own sake, such that we will feel better if we could just "dump" our emotions on someone. By the Spirit, we bring our anger, fear, and grief before God in order that we may be seen by God. And being seen by God leads to transformation. I wrote this in a CarePages entry a few weeks after the diagnosis.

A recent thought I've had about prayer emerges from living with the Psalms. On the one hand, a frequent theme in the Psalms is to seek the face of God, to "taste and see that the LORD is good" (Ps. 34:8). Yet, surprisingly, one of the most significant images related to sight is not about our own *seeing* but our *being seen* by God, by the face of God. This is seen both in lament (e.g., "How long will you hide your face from me?" [Ps. 13:1]) and in petition ("O that we might see some good! Let the light of your face shine on us, O LORD!" [Ps. 4:6]). We are to seek the face of the Lord, but it is not just about what our "eyes" take in. It is about how we are seen.

We live in a day when "being seen" can often have a negative sense: in an age of social media, there are incentives to simply "be seen" by others as having an exciting, adventurous life. But "being seen" is a major feature of human identity. I recall how in high school I felt like a different person when I was around my friends in the debate squad from when I was around my peers in, say, gym class. I acted from a different script.

In a much more powerful way—a way created and opened up by God's Spirit—praying together for a common purpose is a matter not just of "seeing" together but of "being seen" by God together. We're

42

not the heroes in the script of prayer. We praise and bless God, we lament, we petition. We pray, "Thy kingdom come, Thy will be done." It's all about God's face shining on us and being *seen* by God together. But in the light of the radiance of the Triune God, we start to act in a new reality, a new drama, a new script where we taste and see what it means to pray—in this situation—"Thy kingdom come." Thank you for praying with me, in this particular case of cancer, "Thy kingdom come."

Thus, prayer is powerful—but not because our own action is powerful in itself. It is powerful because the Triune God is the hero of the drama of prayer, not us. We bring our whole selves before God, and in that process we are seen by the almighty God and are able to apprehend our new identity in light of his promises. In lament we are confused, angry, and grieving people. But we are not just that. We have been given the script of the Psalms for playing our part in the drama: we are confused, angry, and grieving people who have been given the privilege of crying out to the Lord as his covenant people. Indeed, we are actors who have been clothed with Christ by the Spirit in the theater of God's drama. Because of this, we can openly admit our confusion, anger, and grief without worrying that it will be the last word about who we are. For before the face of God, the last word about our identity is none other than Jesus Christ and our life in him. Following the script of the psalmists, our disoriented affections are redirected by the Spirit, and our trust is directed toward the covenant Lord.

The Way of Lament: Discerning the Pattern of the Psalmists

How does this process take place? The pattern and structure of this process is apparent in the Psalms themselves. For psalms of lament, the pattern looks like this: coming before the almighty Lord, laying open our emotions and complaints before him, and then openly declaring trust in his promises. Psalm 13 gives a brief but quite typical example of a psalm of lament.[6] The first two verses begin by bringing an invocation and complaint to the Lord.

> How long, O LORD? Will you forget me forever?
>> How long will you hide your face from me?
> How long must I bear pain in my soul,
>> and have sorrow in my heart all day long?
> How long shall my enemy be exalted over me?

These verses come to God with a complaint, but also trust: the psalmist is bringing his burden to the Lord, after all. References to God "forgetting" and "hiding" his face are inversions of attributes of God frequently referenced in the Psalms—that God remembers his covenant people and will shine his face on them. In the midst of a crisis with "pain" and "sorrow"—and the triumph of the psalmist's enemies—the psalmist brings this before the Lord, protesting that this is not the way things are supposed to be.[7]

The psalmist continues with a petition, a cry for help.

> Consider and answer me, O LORD my God!
>> Give light to my eyes, or I will sleep the sleep of death,
> and my enemy will say, "I have prevailed";
>> my foes will rejoice because I am shaken. (13:3–4)

The psalmist cries for deliverance, seeing God as the One who can provide the vital help. "Consider," "answer," "give"—the petition is for God to show his faithfulness in the midst of this crisis. In this passage, the psalmist gives a motivating reason for God to act "or I will sleep the sleep of death," all rooted in the plea for God to show his mercy and faithfulness.

> But I trusted in your steadfast love;
>> my heart shall rejoice in your salvation.
> I will sing to the LORD,
>> because he has dealt bountifully with me. (vv. 5–6)

Like most psalms of lament, this psalm moves from laments and petitions to a clear expression of trust—trust in God's "steadfast love" and "salvation." Then, the final verse gives an anticipation of the praise of God for his deliverance; once the Lord has provided his deliverance, the psalmist will "sing to the LORD" about his merciful work.

However, this does not mean that the psalmist's external situation—that which is causing the pain, confusion, or anger—has changed between the petition in verse four and the ending statement of trust. To the contrary, psalms of lament "make that move *without ever telling us that the external situation has changed for the better.*"[8] The psalm provides a pattern that God uses to bring our tears before God and to move us toward deeper trust in the midst of those tears. The final declaration of trust is not dependent on having one's situation fixed or immediately "resolved." Indeed, trust in God's promises underlies the whole of the psalms of lament. For while the psalms of lament are psalms of confusion, anger, and fear, they are also psalms of hope— prayers that come before God in hope, making a plea for him to show himself faithful to his promises.

Lament as a Form of Praise

As strange as it sounds, prayers of lament in a biblical pattern are actually a form of praise to God and an expression of trust in his promises. But some Christians wonder how it could be faithful to complain to God. What about Paul's admonition to "rejoice in the Lord always" in Philippians 4:4? Why should Christians lament, after all, if God's promises are fulfilled in Jesus Christ? Isn't it possible for lament to be a sign of unfaithfulness, self-pity, and ingratitude?

Laments can be misdirected. Some may assume that all we need to do is to vent our emotions and expose them to the light of day. Or others may distort lament by using it as a form of self-pity; for some, it could just be a way to complain about interruptions in their comfortable, middle-class lifestyle, without an eye toward seeking God's kingdom in those circumstances. There are a number of ways in which it is possible

45

to lose sight of the end, or purpose, toward which biblical lament is directed: moving in our grief, confusion, and protest toward trust and thanksgiving in God and his promises. Indeed, we can see something about the nature of this end in Philippians 4:6: "In everything by prayer and supplication with thanksgiving let your requests be made known to God." Pray to God, present your petitions to God—but with thanksgiving. This is also a feature of the vast majority of psalms of lament. A few months after my diagnosis, I reflected on this tight linkage between lament, praise, and thanksgiving in my CarePages.

> Blessed be the LORD,
>> who has not given us
>> as prey to their teeth.
> We have escaped like a bird
>> from the snare of the fowlers;
> the snare is broken,
>> and we have escaped.
> Our help is in the name of the LORD,
>> who made heaven and earth. (Ps. 124:6-8)

In praying with the psalmist, I often notice how praise, petition, and lament are tightly woven together. Psalm 124 struck me for the way in which it gives exalting praise to God in the midst of distress that evokes petition and lament. The psalmist praises "the LORD, who made heaven and earth" while speaking of being nearly torn "as prey to their teeth" and caught in "the snare of the fowlers." In this context, our God is a deliverer. As we seek to be seen by the face of the Lord—on the issues in this CarePages and the other areas of our life—my hope is that our petitions can be less of a long "wish list" to God and more of a time of fellowship with the One who first and foremost deserves our praise. In light of the messes we find ourselves in, this God is also our Deliverer in times of trouble.

One challenge of the cancer journey is that of envy. This is common for folks with cancer, especially when diagnosed at a young age. For

46

me, the questions popped into my head after my diagnosis: Why me? Why now, rather than three or four decades from now? How can other people my age "take for granted" their upcoming decades, when those years are in a fog for me? At times, I would see a person who is seventy or eighty years old and think, "Why do they get to live that long?" "What are the chances that I could possibly live that long?"

This is a place where I find the Psalms particularly helpful. On the one hand, the Psalms are honest about our fears, our feelings of injustice. They don't patch it over with sentimentality. However, they do not end there. They go to a much more life-giving place—bringing all of that before the face of God. And God is much more wondrous and compelling than all of our troubles. Without denying the loss, when we pray with the psalmist we can begin to see the gifts that the Lord, Maker of heaven and earth, has given each of us—tremendous, daily gifts to which we can only properly respond with gratitude. Gratitude and praise to God do not make the lament and petitions go away. We only fully enter lament when we realize that we're not just expressing ourselves to a human observer but bringing our burdens before the Lord, the Creator, the Almighty, who—in light of our distress—is our Deliverer.

Praise, petition, and lament in the Psalms are all tightly woven together in prayers that help us recognize and rest in God's promises. As John Calvin says in his Psalms commentary, "It is the word of God alone which can first and effectually cheer the heart of any sinner. There is no true or solid peace to be enjoyed in the world except in the way of reposing upon the promises of God."[9] The Psalms bring our whole life before God—in happiness and grief, in joy and bitterness—and focus our eyes on God's promises.

However, we can also consider another question. Since the promises of God are fulfilled in Jesus Christ, does this displace a role for lament for Christians? While I heartily affirm with Paul that in Christ "every one of God's promises is a 'Yes'" (2 Cor. 1:20), we have to consider why Paul and other New Testament writers repeatedly incorporate the language of lament in speaking about the present Christian life. "We groan, longing to be clothed with our heavenly dwelling" (2 Cor. 5:2); the Spirit intercedes "with sighs too deep for words" (Rom. 8:26); for "we ourselves, who have the first fruits of the Spirit, groan inwardly while we wait for adoption" (Rom. 8:23). God's promises *are* fulfilled in Christ, but God's kingdom *will* come in fullness in the future, when his reign is uncontested—until then, we lament, crying out with Revelation 22:20, "Come, Lord Jesus!" God's promises come to us from the future, thus our trust in God takes the form of hope: "For in hope we were saved" (Rom. 8:24). Groaning, lament, and longing go together when we trust in a God who promises. When God promises to Moses to deliver the Israelites from Egypt, Moses asks for God's name. YHWH replies, "I AM WHO I AM"—or, as Brevard Childs argues, "I will be who I will be," with the sense of ongoing action (Exod. 3:14). For in this, "God announces that his intentions will be revealed in his future acts."[10] Those who trust in a God who promises already have promises that apply to the present, but they always live in hope. In the same way, the groaning and lamenting of Christians in the New Testament is an expression of hope and trust in God's promises, the promises that are embodied in none other than Jesus Christ himself, who will come again to finally set things right, "to judge the living and the dead."[11]

Thus, there is an underlying hope to psalms of lament that is a form of trust and praise—a lament and hope reflected in the New Testament as well. But what about Psalms 39 and 88, which do not end with the conventional declaration of trust and praise? "Hear my prayer, O LORD, and give ear to my cry. . . . Turn your gaze away from me, that I may smile again, before I depart and am no more" (Ps. 39:12–13). A few things deserve to be said. First, by the very invocation and complaint to God, there is a trust displayed in God. The psalmist calls on God to act, and by inverting God's promises—saying that the current mess makes God's promises seem as if they are *not* true—the psalmist gives God the challenge to be who he promises to be. For in the Psalms, "praise is a double-edged sword," involving "taking God at his word." Thus, thanks is given when God's loving faithfulness is displayed, and protesting lament is used when God's faithfulness is not apparent in the circumstances.[12] Moreover, the fact that Psalms 39 and 88 are in the biblical canon gives us hope that God can handle our hardest pleas and protests. Total despair would not invoke God's presence. Total despair—with no hope at all—does not pray. Yet even the most despairing protests of the Psalms still bring their pleas before God. Indeed, the book of Psalms, about one-third of which is composed of lament psalms, has the Hebrew name *Tehillim*, "Praises." Even the most shocking psalms expressing outrage, fear, and despair are doing so *before God*—and that is praise.

The Theological Heart of the Psalms

Seeing the Psalms as a whole as various prayerful responses to God's promises can allow us to see a core theological assumption that all 150 psalms share: a confession that the Lord is a God of *hesed*, of "loving faithfulness." As Rolf and Karl Jacobson have argued, for all of the Psalms "both God's character and God's characteristic actions are defined by this word: *hesed*."[13] This term, "hesed," variously translated, refers to the Lord's covenantal, steadfast love, faithfulness, and kindness promised to his people Israel. The term is widespread in the Psalms, along with the similar term *emet* ("loving faithfulness").[14] God's covenantal love is shown in his act of creation, in delivering his people, and in his ongoing covenant faithfulness.[15] The Psalms repeatedly celebrate God's loving faithfulness in the giving of the torah (law) and in his promised presence in the temple. The term *hesed* occurs 130 times in the Psalms, including the refrain in each of the twenty-six verses of Psalm 136, praising the Lord "for his steadfast love endures forever." Thus, the psalms of lament come before the Lord in expectation of God's *hesed*, and when God's lovingkindness does not appear to be evident, the psalms of lament complain to God on the grounds of his own covenant promise. The characteristic pattern of the psalm of lament, then, is mirrored in other forms of psalms: psalms that take the form of hymns of praise exalt the loving faithfulness of God's character by testifying to all of his gracious works;[16] psalms of thanksgiving have a similar structure to the psalms of lament—they recall a crisis—but rather than making petition, they recall how the Lord delivered the psalmist from the pit, and offer praise.[17] Again and again the psalmists appeal to God's *hesed*—the Lord's promises to be a faithful covenant partner to his people. Whether celebrating clear signs of God's faithfulness, confessing sin before a God who will faithfully forgive, lamenting to God in the midst of crisis, or recalling God's deliverance, a conviction that God acts as the Lord who has bound himself in covenant love is at the theological center of the book of Psalms.

What about those oh-so-hard-to-pray psalms, which call down curses on the psalmist's enemies? Again, the key is that this rage is brought before the covenant Lord. In praying these psalms, we bring anger before God in its most raw form, before we have carefully reshaped it or internally beaten it down—work that we would like to do ourselves. Rather than seeking retribution on his own, the psalmist cries out to God, bringing anger before the God of covenantal justice. In the words of Miroslav Volf, in the psalms of cursing, "*rage belongs before God . . .* not in the reflectively managed and manicured form of a confession, but as *a pre-reflective outburst from the depths of the soul.* This is no mere cathartic discharge of pent up aggression before the Almighty who ought to care. Much more significantly, by placing unattended rage before God we place both our unjust enemy and our own vengeful self face to face with a God who loves and does justice."[18] With God's promise of covenantal faithfulness at the center, God uses the whole book of Psalms to transform the affections, perceptions, and actions of his people. We don't need to get our life in order before we pray the Psalms. God acts through them. For "even while we are still in our anger, the cursing psalms are the vehicle whereby we yield to God our own claim to vengeance," since appeal is made to God's action (not our own) in response.[19] Indeed, in the words of one extended psalm of cursing, the psalmist cries, "Help me, O LORD my God! Save me according to your steadfast love. Let them know that this is your hand; you, O Lᴏʀᴅ, have done it" (Ps. 109:26–27). The psalmist cries out on the basis of the *hesed* of the Lord and asks for God to do justice rather than leaving it to the psalmist's own hands to give just deserts. Whether in praise, thanksgiving, lament, or the call for God's justice in the form of cursing, the Psalms move us through our kaleidoscope of emotions toward an ongoing trust in the faithful Lord of the covenant.

Praying the Psalms as a People United to Christ

This overarching theme of the Lord's covenant faithfulness helps explain why as Christians we believe that there are various petitioners who have prayed and who continue to pray the Psalms. As I noted in chapter 1, Bonhoeffer explains how the original psalmist in Israel prayed the Psalms; as an individual, I pray the Psalms; and as a church, we pray the Psalms, joining with others around the world and through the ages. But how is it that the individual Christian and the corporate Christian community join in with the prayers of David and other Israelites? On what grounds do we, as Christians, join the psalmist in praying to God as our own covenant Lord? We can do so with confidence because the Holy Spirit has united us to Jesus Christ, and we pray as ones who belong to him. We pray as ones who are baptized in the name of the Triune God and confess that Jesus is Lord. This same Jesus is the fulfillment of the covenant *hesed* of Yʜᴡʜ, the embodiment of God's torah and temple, the great High Priest who also prays the Psalms; he is the "climax" of the covenant, the true Israel acting in his own person, displaying the steadfast, covenantal love of the Father.[20]

In his exposition of the Psalms, Augustine speaks eloquently about reading the Psalms as ones who have been united to Jesus Christ, the Son of God.

> God could have granted no greater gift to human beings than to cause his Word, through whom he created all things, to be their head, and to fit them to him as his members. He was thus to be both Son of God

51

and Son of Man, one God with the Father, one human being with us. The consequence is that when we speak to God in prayer we do not separate the Son from God, and when the body of the Son prays it does not separate its head from itself. The one sole savior of his body is our Lord Jesus Christ, the Son of God, who prays for us, prays in us, and is prayed to by us. He prays for us as our priest, he prays for us as our head, and he is prayed to by us as our God.[21]

When we pray, we do not pray alone. We pray in and through Jesus Christ, the covenantal priest who "holds his priesthood permanently, because he continues forever. Consequently he is able for all time to save those who approach God through him, since he always lives to make intercession for them" (Heb. 7:24–25). We do not pray alone, for "when we cry, 'Abba! Father!' it is that very Spirit bearing witness with our spirit that we are children of God, and if children, then heirs, heirs of God and joint heirs with Christ—if, in fact, we suffer with him so that we may also be glorified with him" (Rom. 8:15–17). When I was praying on the treatment table that "I can do all things through Christ who strengthens me," I was not praying alone. The Spirit was bearing witness to my spirit that I belong to Jesus Christ. And my brother in Christ who was watching me clench the table in pain was praying as well. Indeed, we never pray the Psalms, or any other prayers, alone. We do so as ones who are united to Christ and, as the Father's adopted children, to the church. We do so by the Spirit, who not only enables words of praise and thanksgiving but "intercedes with sighs too deep for words," for while we confess God's loving faithfulness, in this current time we "groan inwardly while we wait for adoption, the redemption of our bodies" (Rom. 8:26, 23).

We are in Christ—we pray in and through him, the Man of Sorrows, who wept for Lazarus and told his disciples at Gethsemane, "I am deeply grieved, even to death" (Matt. 26:38; Mark 14:34). He cried out in lament on the cross from Psalm 22, "My God, my God, why have you forsaken me?" Whether we are dealing with sharp pain as in a bone marrow biopsy or the more dispersed pain of sadness about a diagnosis or another loss, we belong to a Savior, Jesus Christ, who knows human suffering and grief. Both the psalmist and Jesus show us that it is not irreligious to cry out in pain before God, to lament, to grieve. It is an act of faith and trust. For Jesus displayed perfect trust in the covenantal faithfulness of the Father in his life and in his prayers, which continue on our behalf. This faithfulness took the form of petitioning to the Father in the garden to "let this cup pass from me," but also yielding in prayer, saying, "yet not what I want but what you want" (Matt. 26:39). Christ's faithfulness involved lamenting on the cross as one who feels forsaken, yet also hoping in God's lovingkindness confessed in Psalm 22, as we will further explore in chapter 9. Moreover, as Luke's Gospel highlights, Christ's faithfulness also involved calling out in trust and intimacy to God in his final words, "Father, into your hands I commend my spirit" (Luke 23:46). As Christians, we belong to the true Covenant Partner, the true Human Being who laments, petitions, and praises, both displaying and trusting the loving, covenantal *hesed* of God. As we join Christ in prayer in the midst of our tears of pain, anger, and confusion, we grow in trust in God's loving faithfulness and our identity as adopted children of the Father. By God's Spirit, as individuals and as the body of Christ, we grow into the image of Jesus Christ.

4

Lamenting to the Almighty

*Discerning the Mystery of
Divine Providence*

At times, I've sensed that there must be a reason that this cancer has hit me. Even if it's not a good reason—even if I am to blame—I wanted to know the reason. Did I neglect my health in some way, so that I'm getting my due with this cancer? Did I get this rare cancer as a test of my faith? If so, what happens if I fail the "test"? Against my better instincts, at certain moments I felt I'd rather have a reason that explains *why* I have been stricken with this lethal cancer at my young age than leave it as an open question.

Within a week of diagnosis, I found myself in the office of one of the pastors at my church. "I've received prayer from a lot of friends since the diagnosis," I said. "I appreciate the prayer and the support. But when people pray for 'complete healing' or a 'cure,' I can't fully enter in. I'm not even sure what they are praying for or what that would look like, and I feel guilty about that." Those praying for "complete healing" had not been in the room with me when the oncologist explained that the cancer is incurable—it may go into remission, but "it *will* come back," the doctor insisted. On the one hand, I am fine with people praying that my oncologist will be proven wrong. But on the other hand, would they be praying for a "complete cure" if I was eighty-five and struggling with dementia? If not, what puts me in a different category from the elderly dementia patient?

But my worry went deeper.

I continued, "I believe that God can and does heal, though I don't think he always chooses to. I also believe that God's ordinary way of working is through means, like doctors and medicine. But although I'm embarrassed to admit it, here's my worry: what if I'm not healed because I don't have enough faith? What if Neti and Nathaniel lose their dad because he didn't have enough faith?" There was an awkward silence. The pastor started to say, "Well, from my reading of Scripture, I don't think that's how God works. . . ." With a breaking voice, I cut him off. "I agree with you in the biblical exegesis. But I'm at the end of my rope. I'm wondering, what if I'm wrong? Should I try to muster up the faith that I could be cured, just in case God isn't healing me because of a lack of faith?" Another long pause. I knew the answer. While there were issues being raised about petitionary prayer that we will explore more in later chapters, this moment was about something different: if I am not healed, will that be a sign of God's punishment for a lack of faith?

Here is the theology of retribution again from the book of Job (as chap. 2 explored). This is a poisonous variation on the mechanistic retribution theology of Job's friends: faith is rewarded with healing, while the lack of healing is (retrospectively) a sign of a lack of faith. I was tempted—not out of trust but out of servile fear—to wager that God was predictable, able to be manipulated, rather than a God of his word. In this situation, trust in God meant continuing to petition, to trust—but not as a wager based on what I would get out of it. To fear the God of the health-and-wealth gospel is to fear God for my own gain rather than fearing God "for nothing" in return (in the words of Job 1:9). Indeed, this would be trusting in God as a vending machine, which is not really trusting God at all.

56

And yet, the questions sting. Why did I get this life-threatening cancer? For no reason accessible to me. Why did Job suffer? In spite of the fact that God himself appeared to respond to Job's plea, Job was given no reason accessible to him. Why does the psalmist suffer and cry out? Some psalms offer repentance to God. "Wash me thoroughly from my iniquity, and cleanse me from my sin" (Ps. 51:2). But the vast majority of lament psalms do not assume that God is punishing or disciplining for sin through the suffering. Why does the lamenting psalmist suffer? For no reason accessible to the psalmist. It can be difficult to leave these raw questions open. In some ways, it would be easier to succumb to false "answers" like those I was considering in my pastor's office. But that is not the path that the book of Job or the psalmists take. Indeed, as Paul speaks of the place of "groaning" for the new creation in the Christian life, and as Jesus laments in the Gospels, we see that the Father of Jesus Christ does not silence our questions of lament. Instead, the love and power of the covenant Lord is mysteriously displayed to those who offer such open questions in trust. Yet while God is the almighty, sovereign Lord, sometimes we need to trust in the dark as we wait for the fulfillment of God's promises in the dawn.

Cries of Lament: Holding God Responsible to His Covenant Promises

The biblical practice of leaving suffering as an open question before God can be difficult to maintain, particularly as we consider the providential care and power of God. Yet leaving the problem of suffering and evil as an open question is essential if we are to affirm Scripture's testimony about who God is and who we are. It enables us to embrace two sides of the psalmists' testimony: that the covenant God of Israel is the sovereign and benevolent King, and that, because of God's covenant promises, we are to thank the Lord when we see his promises come to fruition and complain to him in lament when we do not. If we knew the "reason" God allows the calamity, there would be no place for ongoing lament.

Yet, as the New Testament testifies, lament is part of the Christian life until the final kingdom comes.

Underlying the psalmist's lament is the confidence that the God of Israel is King—Y<small>HWH</small> is the sovereign, covenant Lord.

> The L<small>ORD</small> is king; let the peoples tremble!
>> He sits enthroned upon the cherubim; let the earth quake!
> The L<small>ORD</small> is great in Zion;
>> he is exalted over all the peoples.
> Let them praise your great and awesome name.
>> Holy is he!
> Mighty King, lover of justice,
>> you have established equity;
> you have executed justice
>> and righteousness in Jacob. (Ps. 99:1–4)

The knowledge and power of the sovereign Lord are not limited like that of human beings. "Even before a word is on my tongue, O L<small>ORD</small>, you know it completely. You hem me in, behind and before, and lay your hand upon me" (Ps. 139:4–5). This and countless other passages in the rest of Scripture testify that God is the one sovereign King. And they represent a key theological assumption for the psalmists. As one Old Testament scholar states, "This God [of the Psalms] has uncompromised dominion over *all* of life, ordering the lives of his people." And yet, "It is faith in a sovereign God that causes confusion" in psalms of lament. "Why does an all-powerful king suddenly and inexplicably no longer bless, no longer order life, and no longer hold things together? If a person did not believe that God was sovereign, there would be no cause for lament."[1] It is precisely out of trust that God is sovereign that the psalmist repeatedly brings laments and petitions to the Lord.

Thus the psalms of lament are not like the grumbling of the Israelites in the wilderness, who displayed a lack of faith in God's promises. Because of their faith in God's sovereignty, the psalmists have high expectations of God; because they take God's promises seriously, they lament and protest when it seems that God is not keeping his promises.

They assume that "if God is responsible for blessing, God is also responsible for the lack of blessing."[2] They avoid the extreme positions of saying that a lack of blessing must be from a lack of faith (like in my opening example), or even from Satan. God is sovereign, and God is good—thus to be trusted in prayer. But God is also to blame, in some sense, when crisis occurs and his promises look like they are unfulfilled.

In what sense, exactly, does the psalmist blame God amid crisis? The psalmist does not "blame" God in the sense of a judge who blames a defendant as he delivers a verdict and dismisses the defendant from the courtroom. If the psalmists had already decided the verdict—that God is indeed unfaithful—they would not continue to offer their complaint. They would have a solution to the problem of evil that silences the questions of lament: that God is not trustworthy, not wholly good. Instead the psalmists blame God in the interrogative, with raw, unanswered questions that cling to the hope of God's covenant promise: Why am I in this crisis if the Lord's covenant promise is true? In the context of covenant fellowship, God's people can cry out to their covenant Lord—in complaint, even in protest and open-ended blame—until God shows his faithfulness according to his covenant promise.

Thus, unlike Israel's polytheistic neighbors, Israel had to live in the midst of this mystery with the problem of evil as an open question. For Israel's neighbors in the ancient Near East, adversity and blessing could be seen as the result of different, competing deities.[3] But this is categorically different from Job, the Psalms, and other biblical books. God is sovereign. God is not evil—God is good. In the book of Job, even the accuser, Satan, is limited by God's power.

Rather than rationalistically "solving" the problem by limiting God's power or denying his goodness, the psalmist lives in the midst of the open question by praying God's promises back to God in complaint and lament. The eyes of the psalmist are on the Lord's scriptural, covenantal promises, holding him responsible in the midst of crisis.

> Why do you hold back your hand;
> why do you keep your hand in your bosom? (Ps. 74:11)

59

Rouse yourself! Why do you sleep, O Lord?
　　Awake, do not cast us off forever! (Ps. 44:23)

My God, my God, why have you forsaken me? (Ps. 22:1)

As Glen Pemberton points out, all of these questions of lament are based on God's promises elsewhere in Scripture.[4] The first lament wonders, Why is the Lord's hand of power, which was promised to Moses for deliverance from Egypt, being withheld? "So I will stretch out my hand and strike Egypt with all my wonders that I will perform in it; after that he will let you go" (Exod. 3:20). Why is God's hand being "held back" this time around?

The second lament asks, Why does the Lord not appear to be acting like the covenantal God of deliverance, appearing to "sleep" like the all-too-human god of Baal on Mount Carmel? The psalmist asks the Lord to show that he is *not* like Baal. And Elijah jeers Baal's prophets, "Cry aloud! Surely he is a god; . . . perhaps he is asleep and must be awakened" (1 Kings 18:27).

The third lament, asking why the Lord has rejected his people in Psalm 22, pivots on the covenant promise that Moses reminded the Israelites of before they entered the Promised Land: "It is the LORD who goes before you. He will be with you; he will not fail you or forsake you" (Deut. 31:8). Why does the psalmist feel forsaken if this is a covenant God who will not forsake his people?

Are the psalmists denying these promises from Exodus, Deuteronomy, and 1 Kings? No. Their open questions are prayers of hope in these promises. They refuse to accept a tamed, domesticated God who is not as powerful or as good as these covenantal promises indicate. As they do so, they are not fatalists who simply say, "This is the way things are supposed to be" when crisis hits. They live in the genuine, biblical, mysterious paradox of serving a good, almighty God who holds the world in his hands even when the world seems to be spiraling out of control.

Even psalms of thanksgiving, which celebrate the Lord's deliverance from crisis, hold the Lord responsible in the midst of the calamity as they give thanks for his deliverance. Before breaking into thanksgiving,

60

the psalmist declares in Psalm 66, "You brought us into the net; you laid burdens on our backs; you let people ride over our heads; we went through fire and through water" (v. 11). After this declaration that God was responsible for these "burdens" for being caught in the net, thanksgiving is offered: "Yet you have brought us out to a spacious place" (v. 12). In a similar way, before recalling the lament in Psalm 30, the poet simply says, "You hid your face; I was dismayed" (v. 7). Yet, as in Psalm 66, not only the crisis but the deliverance is attributed to God. "You have turned my mourning into dancing; you have taken off my sackcloth and clothed me with joy, so that my soul may praise you and not be silent. O LORD my God, I will give thanks to you forever" (30:11–12). The poet's thanksgiving is a recollection of God's mighty acts of deliverance—deliverance from "death" and "the Pit" (30:9). Yet thanks is given in a way that bows before mystery rather than trying to overpower it. At the heart of both thanksgiving and lament is *hope* in a God who is both good and almighty—the Lord who is faithful to his promises.

The psalmist's hope is not in a God of wish fulfillment. As these thanksgivings testify, God does not always act how the poet wants. And although God is good, God is not so distant from evil that he simply mourns with the sufferer, unable to do anything about it. The poet blames God in the calamity and thanks God for deliverance, all on the basis of the Lord's covenant promises. God does not promise cures from cancer, a new car, or a big house; the God of Scripture is not a means to be used for our desired ends. God is the King. And even when the psalmist has to wait in silence, in darkness, it is the sovereign God of covenant promises for whom the poet waits. "I wait for the LORD, my soul waits, and in his word I hope; my soul waits for the Lord more than those who watch for the morning, more than those who watch for the morning" (Ps. 130:5–6). Waiting in the darkness of "the depths" (v. 1), the psalmist who breaks forth in lament and thanksgiving does not wait for an idol but for the God of his own Word, for "in his word I hope." As we wait for the Lord, we should be content to confess the illuminating mystery of God's Word rather than a God who is an idol—an idol constructed to avoid the paradoxes of God's revelation through Scripture.

A Dangerous Extreme: Fatalism

In confessing the mystery of God's providence, contemporary Christians are often tempted by two extremes, both of which may appear to be faithful to biblical teaching at first but fall flat in the end. The first properly observes that God is active in the world and that the psalmist implicates God in the midst of crisis. From this, contemporary Christians conclude that God is the sole actor in history—that every event comes in a *direct, unmediated* way from God. Yet this view is one-sided: while the psalmist implicates God, the poet also blames other humans as a cause of calamity ("many are those who would destroy me, my enemies who accuse me falsely" [Ps. 69:4]). For the psalmist, the enemies act against the way of God—God is not the *only* active agent in the world. Victims of oppression should not fatalistically say, "This is the way things *must* be—God must desire for my situation to be as it is." Instead, they can cry out with the psalmist that, based on God's promise, this is *not* the way things ought to be. When we pray for victims of abuse and ongoing injustice in its various forms, we can join the psalmist in lament, petition, and protest: a young woman is sexually abused by a neighbor but is filled with too much shame to tell anyone; an African American man is repeatedly subjected to racial profiling and discrimination in his community. Again and again, the Psalms return to God's covenant promise to hear the cry of his people in oppression and injustice. The psalmist testifies, "The LORD works vindication and justice for all who are oppressed" (103:6). The abused young woman and the stigmatized African American man should not stay silent, but in lament and protest, they—and others with them — can bring their petitions before God, the Deliverer, in a way that goes hand in hand with publicly testifying to the evil that they face: "Rise up, O LORD; O God, lift up your hand; do not forget the oppressed" (Ps. 10:12).

Thus, for the psalmist, God is not the sole actor in the world—there are other creatures who act against the ways of God. Yet the psalmist does not leave it there, as if we should *only* complain to the enemies themselves when we face oppression. The psalmists repeatedly complain *to God*, crying out in lament for deliverance even as they are oppressed by their enemies: "I say to God, my rock, 'Why have you forgotten me? Why must I walk about mournfully because the enemy oppresses me?'" (Ps. 42:9; see also Ps. 10:12; 44:24; 56:1). Moreover, in Psalm 110:1 the Lord promises to Israel's king in the Davidic line to "make your enemies your footstool."[5] Thus, even enemies are in the hand of God, although their evil actions are not the direct, unmediated work of God. All creatures depend on God for their life and strength, and the God who upholds creation also enables creaturely agency. Because of God's sustaining power, God is not the only agent in the world. Moreover, while God is free to heal and to act in whatever way expresses his holy love, the position of seeing God as the *sole* actor in the world overlooks the fact that God ordinarily works through *means*—in a *mediated* way, through people and water and bread and wine.

The tendency to assume that God always acts in direct and immediate ways has been particularly apparent to me since my cancer diagnosis. At times, the same people who prayed for my immediate healing—and made the plea to God that he must answer because of our faith—scolded me when I prayed that God would work through the doctors and the chemotherapy to defeat the cancer. I would ask for prayer that the chemo would effectively combat the cancer, as well as prayer for my family, and for the struggle with cancer to be used for the sake of God's kingdom. Sometimes people prayed this way. At other times, prayers were offered with a sense of frustrated impatience at tying God's work to the human work of doctors and medicine.

Throughout the process, I've shared with others that I don't see my role as being the "prayer police," someone who regulates the way that others pray for me. Yet I was often asked for prayer requests, and when asked, I would give a response that assumed that while God *could* act apart from external means—like medicine—his ordinary way of acting is *through* such means.[6] I made sure to offer praise and thanks to God—not just the doctors—when there were positive results; for it is indeed God working in and through these means, and the proper response is gratitude. Yet some say that it's just a weak accommodation to modern secularism to assume that God works *through* means rather than to expect and pray for a "direct" cure. I disagree. A quotation from John Calvin, hardly a secularist or a deist, is typical of many pre-Enlightenment Christian theologians on this point.

> I can prove that medicine came from God, inasmuch as it is a knowledge of carefully using the gifts of creation, which God gives us according to the necessities to which we are subjected. For, in the same way that God, having subjected our bodies to hunger and thirst, provides us with an ability to eat and drink in order to overcome our need, and, having subjected us to cold and heat, provides us with means of remedying the problem, God equally, having subjected us to maladies, provides us with the capacity to attend to our illnesses. . . . But I say that whoever does not take account of the means which God has ordained does not have confidence in God but is puffed up with false pride and temerity.[7]

Not only does God's providence work through external means like food, drink, heat, and medicine, but it is a prideful act of unbelief to assume that the God of creation simply bypasses these means in providing healing.

This approach leads to what Michael Horton calls "hypersupernaturalistic fatalism" among many contemporary Christians. These Christians "often speak as if God does all things *in their lives* directly, without any instrumental means."[8] They reprove those who speak about God working through medicine, and "in more extreme cases, some believers even excuse their laziness and lack of wisdom or preparation by appealing to God's sovereignty. 'Just pray about it'; 'If God wants it to happen, it will happen.'" They assume that God is active but in a way that leaves humans inactive—for whatever happens, in its particulars, is a "direct and immediate act of God."[9] To use a technical term, this approach sees God's activity in terms of "monocausality": God is the sole cause for what happens in the world, directly and immediately causing each event. This approach fails to recognize the agency of creatures who have a will that is distinct—and often opposed to God. Such a monocausal approach is condemned as an extreme position by a wide range of theologians—patristic, medieval, and Reformation-era, Arminians and Reformed alike. But in contemporary Western Christianity, it is surprisingly common.

An Opposite Extreme: The World Is Not in the Hands of God

It might feel like a solution to counter this fatalistic, monocausal approach would be to say that some events are simply due to chance—that God couldn't have done anything about them anyway. In the midst of a crisis, does it not damage God's reputation to say that God intentionally "allowed" the calamity? Did God desire that I would acquire cancer at the age of thirty-nine? Or even worse, does God desire horrible tragedies, such as the abuse of a child? Surely, the reasoning goes, God is *opposed* to the suffering of the innocent, thus God simply opposes evil and in no way permits or allows it. Why would God allow calamity? It is tempting to give a reason that answers the theodicy question: the calamity took place because of God's own limitations—God must be simply mourning with the sufferer because he couldn't do anything about it. The horrific sufferings in the world are evidence that some things are utterly outside of God's hands of power, for an omnipotent God would never have permitted this.

This may seem faithful—seeking to answer the theodicy question by saying that God is good but not all-powerful. It keeps God's hands clean, his reputation untarnished. Anyone saying that God is implicated in a tragic event is rebuked: "God didn't want this!" Yet it's another extreme that classically rooted theologians from a wide range of Christian traditions have opposed. In my view, its extremism is shown in the fact that it does not take the psalmist's cry seriously—for the psalmist frequently *blames* God in the midst of calamity, as demonstrated above. If God is not almighty, there is no impetus to blame or implicate God. Moreover, rather than keeping the theodicy question open as the psalmists and the book of Job do, it seeks to "answer" it by saying that the calamity was out of God's control anyway.

A few weeks before writing this, I attended a funeral for a six-year-old boy named Oliver, who died of cancer. The family had fought this childhood cancer with boldness for several years, using every treatment available. But after countless tests and many chemo treatments, they ran out of options. Oliver entered home hospice care. One day, an ice cream truck came into the neighborhood, and Oliver's father carried his thin, cancer-ridden son to get an icy treat, passing by our house. Our two-year-old waved happily; our three-year-old stared with wide eyes. That was the last time that we saw Oliver alive.

The funeral was at a Roman Catholic church, and the priest repeatedly said, "God has called Oliver to himself," and "God has chosen to call Oliver to himself at this time." Wow. A part of my heart cried, "Surely not!" We had been praying for Oliver and his family, and all of us were doing everything possible to help fight the cancer, to fight for Oliver's life. But now the priest was confessing that God is sovereign King even in the suffering and death of Oliver. There was a sting to this—implicating God in the struggle with Oliver's cancer and his death at a young age—but also a reassurance. The sting is the theodicy question as an open question. It hurts. The death of a child is not the way things are supposed to be—why did God allow this to happen? Yet the reassurance is that Oliver did not just slip through God's fingers. In life and death, Oliver was in God's hands. With the psalmist, we confess that God deserves praise for his gifts and the blessing of life, and God is implicated even in the calamity of death as well. Oliver was in God's hands, even when we don't understand why this has happened or how this could fit within God's purposes. Nevertheless we trust in the goodness and power of the Almighty, even though the reasons for the suffering are beyond human wisdom.

God's Providence: Sustaining and Governing

In the ancient, medieval, and Reformation-era church, a set of affirmations and distinctions were utilized in the course of biblical exegesis to avoid extreme responses while guarding the central, guiding mystery of God's providential care. Positively, these statements affirmed in various ways that the Triune God not only freely created the world but that God the King continues to sustain and govern the world toward his own good ends. The Westminster Shorter Catechism distills this earlier theology well when it exposits God's works of providence as "His most holy, wise, and powerful *preserving* and *governing* all His creatures, and all their actions" (emphasis added). But how exactly can one affirm God's kingly rule—with his preserving and governing power—without falling into the fatalistic trap of monocausality described above? On the other hand, if one avoids monocausality, how can we avoid a deism that assumes that God takes a "hands off" approach to the world rather than actively preserving and governing his creation?

Thus, with the affirmations that God *preserves* and *governs* his creation, we need further distinctions—not to vanquish God's mystery but to help us to confess and adore the mystery of God's work set forth in Scripture. These terms (described in the next section) were then utilized for centuries in many Protestant confessions and by theologians as well for a range of different positions on providence (Reformed, Arminian, Roman Catholic, etc.). These distinctions do not give us a theodicy explaining God's reason for allowing evil. And like all extrabiblical distinctions, they can be misconstrued or misused. But used wisely, they give us ways to speak about the complexity of God's kingly rule in Scripture, even though the workings of God's providence remain mysterious. God displays active love and care for the whole creation, but in our fallen world this loving action is a mystery that we can confess rather than information we can control.

Recovering Classical Distinctions: A Biblical Mystery, contra Deism and Fatalism

The most basic category is that of *concursus*, which refers to "the simultaneity of divine and human agency in specific actions and events."[10] It seeks to come to terms with the way in which one and the same action can be attributed to human beings and to the work of God in Scripture. For example, when Joseph's brothers sell him into slavery, was this a human act or a divine act? On the one hand, the act of the brothers was a free, contingent act in the biblical narrative. Yet God acts to preserve and govern creation through even that act, as Joseph testifies: "God sent me before you to preserve life" (Gen. 45:5). So, who really sent Joseph into Egypt? A doctrine of concursus provides a way to say that *both* God *and* Joseph's brothers were actors in the event. God is sovereign, and human beings perform responsible, contingent acts. Divine and human agency do not compete with each other—as if God's action would undermine human agency. To the contrary, God's power makes human agency possible. Thomas Aquinas says it this way: God is the "first" or primary cause, "who moves causes both natural and voluntary." Although "free will is the cause of its own movement," it does not necessarily follow that "what is free should be the first cause of itself." A creaturely action can have the providential power of God as a primary cause, yet the creature still has agency that moves freely. Indeed, God "does not deprive their actions of being voluntary: but rather He is the cause of this very thing in them; for He operates in each thing according to its nature."[11] For Aquinas, in the concursus of divine and human action, God actually *empowers* secondary agents to act in freedom. Creatures could not act in voluntary, responsible freedom apart from God's providential power.

A related distinction that helps to explain the nature of divine-human concursus is the *active* and *permissive* will of God.[12] God's "permission" does not mean that God is a passive spectator but that God (mysteriously) chooses to allow sinners to do the evil that is in their hearts: "God gave them up in the lusts of their hearts to impurity" (Rom. 1:24). God permits the accuser, Satan, to bring suffering to Job, even though we still do not know God's reasons. As followers of Christ, we pray for the kingdom to come because although the Triune God is King, his kingship is not uncontested, as it will be one day: "at the name of Jesus every knee should bend, in heaven and on earth and under the earth, and every tongue should confess that Jesus Christ is Lord, to the glory of God the Father" (Phil. 2:10–11). Until the kingship of Jesus Christ, the Lamb of God, is uncontested, we live in a world in which all things that take place are in the governing hands of God. But not all things are "God's will" in exactly the same way—some things God works through his permission, and other things God works through his actively bringing about conformity to Christ's reign by the Spirit's power.

Thus we trust that even though God is not the author of evil, God's governance will bring what was intended as evil to good ends, even as God did with the evil intended by Joseph's brothers; more significantly, God brought redemption through the evil act of the soldiers' crucifixion of Jesus Christ. In contrast, as when Jesus replies to Nicodemus, God's active will is demonstrated in bringing new life that gives eyes to see and ears to hear, for "no one can see the kingdom of God without being born from above" (John 3:3). God's loving desire is for creatures to experience the freedom of life in Christ's kingdom, and the Spirit actively gives eyes and ears to sinners to make this possible. But why do not all believe the gospel when they hear it? Why does God permit ongoing rebellion? As Roman Catholic theologian Matthew Levering suggests, only God knows. Yet "the central aim of the doctrine of permission is to affirm God's love: as it befits infinite Love, God wills only good to his rational creatures."[13] The doctrine of permission holds together the paradox of God's power and God's loving beneficence, even as we are left with the same mystery that Job and the psalmists encountered. Or, in the words of one Reformed confession about the "ordaining" or "willing" of God, "God does not ordain evil in the same way that God ordains good—that is, as something pleasing to God—but as something God hates." Yet God freely permits the evil of creatures, "and in a wonderful way uses [it] for good."[14] God hates evil, yet the world is in God's governing hands to such an extent that we can lament and blame God when he wills to permit evil. We don't know why God permits evil—in general or in our particular circumstances. Yet with the psalmist we can come before a God who is good and trustworthy, powerful and loving, with lament, petition, and praise until Christ's kingdom has fully come.

On Falling Sparrows and Hair: Providence and Chemotherapy

Three months after my diagnosis, I reflected on some key Scripture passages related to providence, finding these distinctions helpful in relation to my cancer journey.

Are not two sparrows sold for a penny? Yet not one of them will fall to the ground apart from your Father. And even the hairs of your head are all counted. So do not be afraid; you are of more value than many sparrows. (Matt. 10:29–31)

At our transplant meeting, I was told that I would lose all of my hair because of the intensive chemo involved in the transplant. Rachel and I decided to go ahead and share with our three-year-old, Neti, that I would lose my hair in a few months because of being sick—though we added that it would eventually come back. Neti has been quite interested in talking about it. While I was driving home with her a few days ago, she brought up the topic, and then said to me reassuringly, "God will give your hair back." Then, in curiosity, she asked, "Will God give you *blue* hair? I hope God gives you *blue* hair!"

Apart from Neti's wish for dada to have *blue* hair, the subject does raise some questions that I've been sorting through recently. In the opening Question and Answer of the Heidelberg Catechism, it says that Christ "watches over me in such a way that not a hair can fall from my head without the will of my Father in heaven; in fact, all things must work together for my salvation."[15] While this confessional statement reflects the truths of a number of different scriptural passages, a key one for the reference to "hair" falling from one's head is the Matthew 10:29–31 passage above. In Matthew 10, Jesus is speaking about sending his followers out as witnesses, warning them that they will face opposition and persecution (vv. 16–23). Yet they need not fear (vv. 26–28); they are not sent out on their own but with the blessing of God's provision and presence. Thus the powerful

70

passage about providence in verses 29–31 above is not in the context of assuring Christians that they will have an easy life or that they are entitled to bypass pain or suffering. Rather, Christ assures us that we need not fear that opposition to our witness to him will finally win out. Moreover, on a more intimate level, neither a sparrow nor a hair "will fall to the ground apart from your Father." The NRSV is quite literal in its rendering here—some other translations try to unpack the phrase a bit more with "outside your Father's care" or "without your Father's will," "consent," or "knowledge." The passages from Matthew and the Heidelberg Catechism point to a providential care that is both reassuring and mysterious. Was it the Father's "will" that I undergo intensive chemo treatment? Did the Father just "consent" to this, given our fallen world in which people get cancer? Or did the Father just "know" that this would take place? Personally, I find a distinction from another confession, the Belgic, to be illuminating here: it speaks about the distinction between God's active will from creation and God's permissive will, given the mess of sin that we are in (Belgic Confession, article 13). The distinction doesn't explain away the mystery, but it gives a way to speak about cancer and the stem cell transplant: it is not God's "will" from the foundations of the earth, yet given our fallen situation it is still within God's hands, still within God's "permission" in some sense, for God can and does use even evils like cancer toward his own good ends. As Joseph says to his brothers about their opposition and betrayal, "You intended to harm me, but God intended it for good to accomplish what is now being done" (Gen. 50:20 NIV).

The Belgic Confession belongs to the Reformed tradition, but it reflects basic features characteristic of most classical approaches to providence in making use of common catholic distinctions in describing God's kingly rule and divine-human concursus. It marks out the extreme positions to be avoided: that "this good God, after creating all things, did not abandon them to chance or fortune," and, on the other hand, "God is not the author of, and cannot be charged with, the sin that occurs." The Confession states that calamity does not just happen to slip through the fingers of God (chance), but neither is God the author of evil or sin. For "nothing can happen to us by chance but only by the arrangement of our gracious heavenly Father, who watches over us with fatherly care, sustaining all creatures under his lordship, so that not one of the hairs on our heads (for they are all numbered) nor even a little bird can fall to the ground without the will of our Father. In this thought we rest, knowing that God holds in check the devils and all our enemies, who cannot hurt us without divine permission and will." The Belgic Confession openly admits that this leaves us with a mystery. But it is a luminous mystery, giving assurance of God's care from his Word even when we don't know the reason he has allowed this crisis. For "we do not wish to inquire with undue curiosity into what God does that surpasses human understanding and is beyond our ability to comprehend. But in all humility and reverence we adore the just judgments of God, which are *hidden* from us, being content to be Christ's disciples, so as to learn only what God shows us in the Word, without going beyond those limits" (emphasis added). The Belgic Confession notes that God discloses his will for Christ's disciples in his Word: in God's law and promise, fulfilled in Jesus Christ, we've been given a new identity, we know whom to trust, we know the path that our affections and actions should take as followers of Christ. Some call this the "revealed will" of God. But at times, when calamity comes, God's will is just "hidden," and we should leave it in his hands. We should not speculate about why God has allowed a disaster in nature to occur at a particular moment or why God has allowed me to have cancer at this particular time. We don't know. But we can put our trust in God's own Word—a trust that manifests itself in lament and thanksgiving, petition and praise.

Caring for the Suffering in Light of a Gracious yet Mysterious Providence

On a practical level, wisely utilizing these distinctions can help Christians who are providing care to the suffering: it gives testimony to God's

72

promise and his providential care without falling into mechanistic views of God's providence, as with Job's "friends" who claimed to calculate what God was doing based on what happened to Job. In giving this kind of testimony to God's providence, we should not rush in and victoriously shout "This is God's will!" in a way that suggests that this calamity was what God intended at the foundations of creation. The Triune God is King, but Christ's kingdom is not yet uncontested. On the other hand, one is not left with the impotent response of saying, "God understands your pain, but couldn't do anything about it." With the psalmist, this approach thanks God for blessing, and also puts the lack of blessing at the door of the Almighty. Suffering and calamity are still under the rule of God, the sovereign King. The sufferer is not subject simply to whims of "chance," yet on the other hand God is not capricious or the author of evil. Instead the sufferer is in the hands of a good and powerful God. A Christian shaped by the Belgic Confession could point the sufferer to the promises in God's Word and assure the sufferer that even in the crisis God is worthy of trust. And in order to truly place God's promises at the center of one's trust, a caretaker would pray psalms of lament as well as psalms of thanksgiving with the sufferer.

In contrast to the modesty of the Belgic Confession about speculating regarding God's reasons for allowing evil, some of my Christian friends often claimed that they could see "the reasons" why particular events had to turn out this way in my cancer journey. I recall expressing gratitude to God for the fact that I could schedule my stem cell transplant in Grand Rapids, about thirty miles from home, rather than having to drive across the state for that multi-month affair. Although the response wasn't in so many words, some responded by basically saying, "God caused you to have cancer and be diagnosed just at this time because his plan is perfect." Whenever there were little breaks that would make my life on chemotherapy a bit more convenient, a response was, "Oh, that's part of God's perfect plan." I agree that these are occasions for which to thank God. But these responses seemed to minimize the calamity of my actual pain and the seriousness of my diagnosis—which were not lessened just because I had a shorter drive or a small break in my treatment. They seemed to assume that God's reasons for allowing suffering were transparent—against the lamenting psalmist, against the book of Job, against Paul, who repeatedly prayed for his "thorn in the flesh" to be removed to no avail.

Yet as followers of Jesus Christ, the crucified Lord, we can have confidence that God works in and through the most calamitous events. In Peter's sermon in Acts 2, he says, "This man, handed over to you according to the definite plan and foreknowledge of God, you crucified and killed by the hands of those outside the law" (v. 23). Yet "this Jesus God raised up," and "God has made him both Lord and Messiah, this Jesus whom you crucified" (2:32, 36). Was the crucifixion of Christ the work of God or the work of the soldiers? It was both. The crucifixion of Christ was not simply a horrific event that happened to slip through God's hands (chance) or an event that completely bypassed human agency (fatalism). A doctrine of concursus helps us articulate the "yes" to both possibilities to which Peter's sermon testifies: it was in "the definite plan and foreknowledge of God," and yet "you" (Peter's hearers), in your own free, contingent act, "crucified" Jesus Christ.[16] It was the will of God—Father, Son, and Holy Spirit—because all three persons desired to save fallen and sinful creatures through the sending of the Son, even to death on a cross, and the sending of the Spirit to unite the Father's adopted people to Christ and one another.

Thanks be to God, for God has reconciled us to him in this act of the cross and resurrection of Christ. Moreover, this Christ is the same one who has been exalted as our priestly mediator—lamenting, petitioning, and praising God—on our behalf. As ones who are in Christ, we can join our own prayers to his, lamenting, petitioning, and praising our good and mighty God.

5

Joining the Resistance

*Lament and Compassionate Witness
to the Present and Future King*

When I was in seminary, I had a friend who was a chaplain at a children's hospital, and he told me about a nurse who was facing what we might call "compassion burnout." She wanted to help people. Perhaps, like many today, she wanted to try to "change the world." But instead, she found herself going into one hospital room after another, providing care for young children with terminal illnesses. They were not likely to live more than a few years, at most. What good was this doing? Was this really "changing the world"?

In a sense, the nurse was facing a different version of Satan's question to the Lord in the book of Job: "Does Job fear God for nothing?" (1:9). Satan was probing—would Job fear God even if God had not "blessed the work of his hands" (1:10)? For the nurse, the question was: Would she serve the sick "for nothing"? Or would she serve them only if her work resulted in the blessing and the positive outcomes that she desired? Would she care for those in need even if it didn't change the world, even if she couldn't extend the lives of these terminally ill children? Christians who seek to serve those in deep need face the question again and again—is it worthwhile to pour out our lives when our efforts don't seem to do any good? I worked on the staff of a homeless shelter for five years; during that time my illusions about heroically "rescuing" the poor were exposed and shattered. Many of our residents struggled with addiction, mental illness, and an economic system that seemed set against them. If I had been motivated by the instrumental outcome—seeing visible transformation in our homeless residents—I would have lasted only a few months rather than five years. Like the nurse, I faced the question: Was I willing to serve the poor "for nothing"? Was I willing to serve the poor even if I couldn't "fix" or "rescue" them?

My chaplain friend responded to the nurse's plight in a striking way: he suggested to her that rather than serving only if she could "change the world," she should continue her service as an act of protest. How do we respond to a world with dying children? He said she should continue her compassionate action as a lament that witnesses that things in this fallen world are not the way they are supposed to be. How do we respond to a world that enslaves women in sex trafficking? We protest, lament, and act with compassion even when we are overwhelmed with the magnitude of the problem. In the words of Paul, we are in a "struggle" against "the powers of this dark world" (Eph. 6:12 NIV) that deal out death and alienation from God and neighbor. We struggle to "stand firm" (v. 13) and bear witness to Jesus Christ, the victor over sin, the devil, and the powers. His victory is secure, but his reign of peace and shalom has not fully come.

From this standpoint, the point of compassionate action is not to "change the world." It is to be faithful and to bear witness in word and deed to a different kingdom: that of King Jesus. As our lips say, "Thy kingdom come," we pray—and act—as revolutionaries who protest against the darkness in this "present evil age" (Gal. 1:4). As Karl Barth says, "The law of prayer is the law of action," for when we pray for God's name to be hallowed and God's kingdom to come, we "cannot come to terms and be satisfied with the status quo."[1] We are to "revolt and fight" against "the disorder which inwardly and outwardly controls and penetrates and poisons and disrupts all human relations and interconnections."[2] Christians have "a binding requirement to engage in a specific uprising," for in "sighing, calling, and crying 'Thy kingdom come,'" Christians enter into a "revolt against disorder."[3] God's good creation is still good, but it has been corrupted and alienated—and God's reign has not reached its final culmination. When the bride of Christ is fully and finally united to her Spouse in the new Jerusalem, then King Jesus will say, "Look! God's dwelling place is now among the people, and he will dwell with them. They will be his people, and God himself will be with them and be their God. 'He will wipe every tear from their eyes. There will be no more death' or mourning or crying or pain, for the old order of things has passed away" (Rev. 21:3–4 NIV). But we're not there yet. Until the day that every tear is dried, death is conquered, and pain is overcome, we pray with our Savior, "Thy kingdom come." In grief. In protest. And in hope. For although the world is in God's hands, things are not the way they are supposed to be.[4] And living as followers of Christ, we lament, give thanks, and hope in relation to God's loving faithfulness, which has practical consequences for how we respond to suffering around us. Hardened hearts can become tender as we hope in God's covenant promises because God is good and powerful, and the suffering, sin, and death around us is not final. Our restless prayers of lament go hand in hand with compassionate protest until Christ's kingdom has fully come.

God Is King, yet We Long for the Final Kingdom

I didn't want or expect cancer. My cancer is an example of what Paul speaks about when he says that "the whole creation has been groaning with labor pains," and "we ourselves, who have the firstfruits of the Spirit, groan inwardly while we wait for adoption, the redemption of our bodies" (Rom. 8:22–23). Having been given the Spirit, we have a taste of our final adoption as God's people, a taste of our final redemption, a taste of the way things are supposed to be. But our bodies ache until the final redemption. We're not there yet.

How could it be that God is the sovereign King, yet we hope for a state of affairs that differs from our own—without pain, suffering, and death? Psalm 96 gives an example of this aspect of God's kingship, repeated frequently in the Psalms. The Lord is King, deserving praise from the whole of creation, thus "sing to the LORD, all the earth." Israel is to "declare his glory among the nations, his marvelous works among all the peoples." Why? Because even when the Lord is not recognized as the universal King of creation, he is. "For great is the LORD, and greatly to be praised; he is to be revered above all gods. For all the gods of the peoples are idols, but the LORD made the heavens." The God of Israel is the Creator of all—the God of Israel is the true King, thus he "is to be revered above all gods" (vv. 1–4).

On the one hand, the psalmist declares that the Lord presently reigns as the true King of the earth, whose reign should be trusted and proclaimed to the nations. "Say among the nations, 'The LORD is king! The world is firmly established; it shall never be moved'" (Ps. 96:10). Yet on the other hand, the psalmist also looks forward to the Lord's uncontested reign. "For he is coming, for he is coming to judge the earth. He will judge the world with righteousness, and the peoples with his truth" (v. 13). The Lord is the true King of the earth. And yet the Lord is coming—to judge as a true King. The judgment spoken about here is the judgment of a righteous King who would set things right; for just as the psalmists repeatedly insist that God is the true kingly ruler of the earth, the Psalms also complain that the wicked are currently flourishing while the righteous perish. Abuse, violence, suffering, and unbelief are all around us.

Thus, as N. T. Wright says, there is "a constant tension in the Psalms between the celebration of creation the way it is and the longing for YHWH to come and put it all right at last. The reason for this tension, so characteristic of all scriptural thought in one way or another, is never explored in itself. The Psalms do not, that is, offer us an answer for 'the problem of evil.'" Rather than loosen the tension by "answering" the problem of evil (by compromising either God's sovereign power or his covenantal love), "the Psalmists again and again celebrate the promise that the creator of the world will renew his creation, 'judging' it in the sense of pronouncing definitively against all that has corrupted and defaced it, and putting it right once and for all."[5]

In the New Testament, Jesus himself lives and prays in the midst of this paradox as well. Jesus announces that the kingdom of God is at hand. And he is "lifted up" as King, as John's Gospel testifies. But his "lifting up" is to the cross. And in the course of that "lifting up," the sin of the world was judged and exposed; for rather than declaring that God is the true, reigning King, the chief priests testified that Caesar was their only king: "Pilate asked them, 'Shall I crucify your King?' The chief priests answered, 'We have no king but the emperor.' Then [Pilate] handed him over to them to be crucified" (John 19:15–16). The chief priests abandoned the repeated testimony of the psalmists and the rest of the Old Testament in order to declare the kingship of one who had the political power to deal out rewards and punishments.

Yet the Triune God shows his love toward creatures who have turned against him as his enemies. Through the cross, Jesus Christ the King is victorious over sin and the devil—over the forces that held his persecutors in bondage. In a mysterious way, Christ takes on sin so that we might take on his righteousness. "For our sake he made him to be sin who knew no sin, so that in him we might become the righteousness of God" (2 Cor. 5:21). Christ's cross is completely sufficient in reconciling us to God; it is a complete victory, a complete judgment of sin, as the psalmist calls for. Yet God's kingship is still not uncontested. Thus Paul says in the same passage, "God, who reconciled us to himself through Christ, and has given us the ministry of reconciliation; that is, in Christ God was reconciling the world to himself, not counting their trespasses against them, and entrusting the message of reconciliation to us. So we are ambassadors for Christ, since God is making his appeal through us; we entreat you on behalf of Christ, be reconciled to God" (vv. 18–20). God has already reconciled sinners like us to himself through Christ and his cross. It is done. It is finished. Yet God is still "making his appeal through us" as ambassadors of the gospel. Like the psalmist, we are to "Say among the nations, 'The LORD is king!'" (96:10). We are to declare God's kingship as fulfilled in Christ. And since God's kingship in Christ is not yet uncontested, our witness involves actions of compassionate protest, like the action of the nurse in the children's hospital, saying, "This is not the way things are supposed to be."

The Ethics of Compassionate Protest versus the Ethics of "This Is the Way Things *Must* Be"

Behind the common expression that God's kingdom is "now but not yet" are paradoxes that run deeply through God's self-revelation in Scripture. God is the only true, sovereign King. Yet what we see around us—a world with cancer and death, sin and alienation—is not his consummated kingdom. The Triune God conquers sin and the devil in the sending of the Father's Son to live, die, and be raised again, all through the Spirit's power. Yet the creation still groans (Rom. 8). We are still in a battle requiring the armor of God "against the rulers, against the authorities, against the cosmic powers of this present darkness, against the spiritual forces of evil in the heavenly places" (Eph. 6:12). God's present reign *is* a kingly, sovereign reign. Sin and the "powers and authority" only have temporary power through permission of the King. For in Paul's words, at "the end," when those who belong to Christ are raised, Christ will have "destroyed every ruler and every authority and power. For he must reign until he has put all his enemies under his feet. The last enemy to be destroyed is death" (1 Cor. 15:24–26). Until then, we protest against God's enemies—death, sin, and the devil—as we bear witness to the present and future King, our God—Father, Son, and Holy Spirit.

Compassionate witness in the mode of lament and protest against sin, death, and the devil does not imply that the problem of evil has been answered. To the contrary, the question of suffering is approached as one that requires our practical response rather than a theoretical answer. Indeed, a theoretical answer to "why this suffering exists" can

80

actually harden our hearts rather than lead us to compassionate action. While working in the homeless shelter, in particular, I could have used scores of reasons to "explain away" the suffering I saw around me: we can't help them because they suffer from mental illness and addiction; we can't help them because they are too broken; we can't help them because they are too stubborn; we can't help them because no one will hire them for a job; we can't help them because they are not healthy enough to *receive* help. All of these reasons point one direction: the present state of the world—with homeless sufferers—is the way things *must* be. Indeed, perhaps some would say that *since* this is the way things are, it's the way that God the King *wants* them to be. But to claim this would be to answer the theodicy question in a way that excuses our indifference and apathy in response to the homeless and other sufferers around us.[6] It would be to miss the radical nature of the Christian faith that prays, "Thy kingdom come on earth," because although God is the sovereign King, his promised reign on earth is not yet fully present.

As atheistic philosopher Friedrich Nietzsche realized with great clarity, how one responds (or does not respond) to suffering says volumes about one's ontology—what one really believes about the world and its present state. Much of Nietzsche's project did not involve arguing directly against belief in God so much as fleshing out the implications of a world in which God was "dead" and the grounds for belief in God had already been undermined. Yet as Nietzsche ironically notes, those who claimed that they had abandoned God still acted as if God were alive. "God is dead; but given the way of men, there may still be caves for thousands of years in which his shadow will be shown. And we—we still have to vanquish his shadow, too."[7] For Nietzsche, one of the most difficult realities to face was that if God is dead, then a compassionate response to the sufferer is nonsense: it implies that there is a world of peace that exists that critiques our present world. That is a shadow of belief in God that needs to be vanquished. In contrast to seeing the present world in light of a world of peace (such as Eden or heaven), Nietzsche argued that violence always was and always will be.

81

To protest against violence is to protest against the way things are—and always will be.

Consequently, in his work *Thus Spoke Zarathustra*, the final "sin" and temptation that Zarathustra faces is that of "pity."[8] Nietzsche thinks that if God is dead, then Zarathustra must learn to ignore the cry of "woe," for "woe entreats: Go! Away, woe!" Woe longs and cries out "for what is farther, higher, brighter."[9] It longs for a world of wishful thinking. In contrast to pity, "joy" does not long for another world, a world without violence. Instead, it "wants recurrence, wants everything eternally the same." Zarathustra teaches that "pity is obtrusive,"—that "whether it be a god's pity or man's, pity offends the sense of shame. And to be unwilling to help can be nobler than that virtue which jumps to help."[10] If the world always was and always will be a world of suffering, then it is nihilistic to "protest" against suffering, to act with pity and compassion.

Nietzsche's portrait is an insightful mirror image presenting the opposite of a Christian perspective on compassion—a view of the world in which there is no lament, no petition to God for things to be different, no pity. Unfortunately, the *action* that he describes—ignoring the sufferer because all pity is "obtrusive"—is frighteningly close to the attitudes of many religious and nonreligious people alike in Western culture today. Much sociological research points toward an increase in this broadly Nietzschean approach to pity. As Ross Douthat notes, in recent decades in the United States "narcissism has waxed" and "empathy has waned." Douthat writes,

> In 2010, researchers at the University of Michigan reported that contemporary college students scored about 40 percent lower than their predecessors in the 1970s on tests assessing their ability to put themselves in other people's shoes. They were more likely than their parents' generation to agree with statements like "other people's misfortunes do *not* usually disturb me a great deal," and less likely to agree with prompts like "I sometimes try to understand my friends better by imagining how things look from their perspective" and "I often have tender, concerned feelings for people less fortunate than me."[11]

82

In other words, lament and compassionate protest against "the way things are" is increasingly seen as unnecessary, as if we are told, "Mind your own business!" The nurse at the beginning of the chapter caring for the needs of terminally ill children would be told, "Don't bother." Extensive interviews with young adults by sociologists Christian Smith and Patricia Snell Herzog show the logic of this even further. While a few stated that they felt an obligation to help those in need, "the majority of those interviewed stated the opposite—that nobody has any natural or general responsibility or obligation to help other people." Ignoring the suffering is a perfectly acceptable response: "They are innocent of any guilt, respondents said, if they ignore other people in need. Even when pressed—What about the victims of natural disaster or political oppression? What about helpless people who are not responsible for their poverty or disabilities? . . . No, they replied."[12] In this form of reasoning, if a person is suffering, it's their own problem. That's the way the world is. And apparently, no sin is greater than that of being "obtrusive"—compassionate action says that this is not the way things are supposed to be. And who is in a place to say that?

Operative Theologies in the West: A God without Paradox, and No Need for Lament

As Smith and colleagues argue in *Lost in Transition*, the studies showing trends like these among teenagers and emerging adults in their twenties reflect larger trends in the overall culture. They are "mirroring back to the older adult world" what has been modeled for them.[13] Thus, "most of the problems in the lives of youth have their origins in the larger adult world into which the youth are being socialized."[14] Moreover, their apathetic refusal to protest against a world of suffering in light of God's coming reign of peace results not from an overt Nietzschean atheism but from a theology that often claims to be Christian. It's a theology that is common among adults as well as teens and emerging adults, and after the most comprehensive study of the religious beliefs of American teens ever performed, it was summed up by sociologists this way:

1. A God exists who created and orders the world and watches over human life on earth.
2. God wants people to be good, nice, and fair to each other, as taught in the Bible and by most world religions.
3. The central goal of life is to be happy and to feel good about oneself.
4. God does not need to be particularly involved in one's life except when God is needed to resolve a problem.
5. Good people go to heaven when they die.[15]

We could make many different kinds of observations about this "creed." The sociologists call it a form of deism because God is not really needed by creatures on a day-to-day basis. It's different from eighteenth-century deism, however, because God shows up to "resolve a problem" when one is in a crisis. Of course, this wish for God to come and resolve our problems is not a prayer of "Thy kingdom come," based on a protest against sin and death in this world. Sin and death are not problems that need to be resolved. Instead, the purpose of religion is to help oneself be "happy and feel good about oneself"—so God helps (only) to those ends. There is no need for a mediator (Christ) to overcome our alienation from God or a Spirit to empower us to good action. Humans are more self-reliant than that, so there is no need for a Triune God to be actively involved in creating, sustaining, and redeeming the world. Instead, "God is something like a combination Divine Butler and Cosmic Therapist: he is always on call, takes care of any problems that arise, professionally helps his people to feel better about themselves, and does not become too personally involved in the process."[16] In several ways, the nerve for lament is cut by this approach: God is good but not particularly involved in creation, thus God cannot be blamed for calamity; moreover, the world itself is just "the way things are." Missing is a longing for the new creation, the fervent prayer of "Thy kingdom come." Thus, it is not surprising that the sociologists

84

noted that "few teens we talked to ended up blaming God for failing them."[17] They are not protesting, lamenting, and hoping for God's new creation.

Sometimes lament is undercut through a form of deism; but as noted in chapter 4, at times Christians in the pew fall into another extreme, which also undercuts the paradoxes of biblical lament: a fatalism that sees every event as a direct, unmediated act of God. A pastor friend of mine was talking to a couple who had just lost a child by a miscarriage. The husband offered no tears. No emotion. Just the words, "It was what God ordained." In this stoic response, he thought he was holding strongly to a "Reformed" view of providence. But he wasn't. He rightly confessed that God is King but missed the place of lament and protest—that the fullness of God's kingdom is not yet here. We yearn and groan for that day. In the words of one Reformed confession, God's permission of sin and evil is not "as something pleasing to God—but as something God hates."[18] God hates for a mother and father to lose a child. God hates the corruption of his good creation. God hates sin. God hates abuse. And so should we. Thus, these two biblical truths go together: the world, even the most difficult circumstances that we face in it, is in the hands of God the King, *and* things are not yet the way they should be. Hence, rather than responding to tragedy like stoics, the Spirit frees us to cry out in grief and protest and hope: "Thy kingdom come," and "Come, Lord Jesus."

On the other hand, another theological movement swings to an opposite extreme that undercuts the paradoxical dynamic of biblical lament as well: open theism. Key advocates such as John Sanders are responding to genuine tragedy in their own lives or the lives of others. And they want to say, rightly, that God hates evil. Indeed, they are right to move against the stoic misinterpretation of classical Christian doctrine in the example above, and the fatalistic, monocausal approaches to providence discussed in chapter 4. But rather than living in the midst of the mystery that God is loving and yet also almighty, thus leading us to lament to a sovereign Lord when his promises appear to be in peril, they let God off the hook: God's power is such that God could not prevent the tragedy. Thus, instead of approaching theodicy as an open question whose answer is beyond human wisdom—with Job, the Psalms, and the classical Christian tradition[19]—it is asserted that God has a general purpose leading to good in giving humans freedom, but in specific instances of tragedy, "God does not have a specific purpose in mind for these occurrences."[20] Specific tragedies are examples of "pointless evil," Sanders asserts—pointless not just from a human perspective but from God's standpoint as well.[21] Crucial for Sanders's approach is his rejection of classical accounts of divine mystery, accommodation, and paradox in his theological method that account for the profound difference between Creator and creature.[22] Thus, he rejects the idea that God could "permit" evil because it implies that God intentionally permits a particular tragedy, which he insists is "pointless."[23] I agree that many tragedies that we encounter look "pointless," and we should not join Job's friends by speculating on God's specific reasons for permitting it. We don't know. But unfortunately, by saying that some evils are pointless *from God's perspective*, Sanders has departed from the message of Job about the limits of human wisdom. He has sought to avoid a biblical paradox by giving a *reason* for the tragedy (i.e., the limits of God's knowledge and power) precisely where we should leave the problem of evil and suffering an open question.

Lament and the Mysterious Middle

While approaches like Sanders's seek to vindicate the goodness of God, they move decisively away from the paradoxes undergirding biblical lament. For if God's knowledge and power are such that God could *not* prevent a specific tragedy, the grounds for biblical lament are cut off at the core. As we explored in some detail in chapters 3–4, biblical psalmists repeatedly blame God for their calamity—even when the sinful actions of human beings are involved—declaring that his sovereign lordship is implicated in their tragic circumstances.

> I was silent; I would not open my mouth,
>   for you are the one who has done this.
> Remove your scourge from me;
>   I am overcome by the blow of your hand. (Ps. 39:9–10 NIV)

Yet the psalmists also pray in hope, bringing their burden before a God who they repeatedly declare is loving and gracious, according to his promise. "O give thanks to the LORD, for he is good, for his steadfast love [*hesed*] endures forever" (Ps. 136:1). Psalmists would have no grounds to blame God in lament if the evil was simply "pointless" to God himself, if God did not actually permit the calamity. Instead of staying at a safe distance from specific tragedies, Scripture presents a narrative "about the messy way in which God has had to work to bring the world out of the mess," N. T. Wright writes. "Somehow, in a way we are inclined to find offensive, God has to get his boots muddy and, it seems, to get his hands bloody, to put the world back to rights. If we declare, as so many have done, that we would rather it not be so, we face a counter question: Which bit of dry, clean ground are we standing on that we should pronounce on the matter with such certainty?"[24] God is deeply involved in the world—so involved that we can and should lament with the psalmist when God's hand permits calamity that seems to call his promises into question. Yet God and his ways are mysterious—we should not bring closure on the mystery of the problem of suffering by denying his almighty power or loving goodness. Instead, as Wright says in a passage that parallels the instincts in the classical tradition in speaking about the power and permission of God, the scriptural narrative tells us "in no uncertain terms that God will *contain* evil, that he will *restrain* it, that he will prevent it from doing its worst, and that he will even on occasion use the malice of human beings to further his own strange purposes."[25] Yet while we affirm this, if we ask the question of why "God will not simply abolish evil from his world," we "are not given an answer."[26]

Thus, these various elements are tightly woven together and interdependent: we affirm the mystery of God's action in the world, protest against a world with sin and death as we hope for God's new creation, and lament to a good and almighty God whose promises we trust. While classical distinctions about providence can be developed in a number of directions, there is a remarkable amount of continuity between classically rooted theologians in the way that they hold together the paradoxes of God's providence, confessing the mystery of a good and almighty God who hates evil yet has the world in his hands. Arminian Methodists such as Thomas Oden, Thomist Roman Catholics such as Matthew Levering, Orthodox theologians such as David Bentley Hart, and Reformed theologians such as Michael Horton all share the basic contours of a classical Christian approach to providence, and each one uses the classical distinctions in a way that keeps biblical lament and thanksgiving alive while undergirding a passionate response to the suffering and alienation of the world.[27]

These classical approaches offer what I call a "mysterious middle" between two extremes: on the one side is fatalistic, monocausal approaches to providence that assume that God always acts directly and immediately; on the other side is the popular deism diagnosed by Smith, as well as the open theism of Sanders, that in different ways keep God and his power too distant from our calamity, blunting rather than testifying to the paradoxes of Scripture. However, not all who loosen the biblical paradox do so by diminishing God's power: John K. Roth, in his "Theodicy of Protest," argues against those who say that evil shows the limits of God's power; they say "God always does the best that God can," but since God is not almighty, he cannot be blamed for evil. Roth counters that a God who is not omnipotent "is hardly worth bothering about."[28] Yet, while affirming God as almighty, he gives up on God's benevolence. Roth protests that "God's saving acts in the world are too few and far between."[29] Stated as a lament in the interrogative mode, Roth's protest could be faithful to the psalmist. We can complain to God with the psalmist, protesting that he does not seem to be fulfilling his promises. Indeed, such laments can lead us to question God's character: C. S. Lewis, after his wife's death to cancer, struggled with questions of whether God is "a good God or the Cosmic Sadist."[30] But in the end, rather than combining the questions of lament with trust in bringing them before the Almighty, Roth declares that "God is everlastingly guilty."[31] By flatly asserting that God is not "wholly good,"[32] Roth has *answered* the problem of evil rather than keeping it as an open question. God is almighty, but calamity takes place because God is not trustworthy. Unfortunately, Roth's approach also cuts off the sufferer from the rationale for ongoing lament, for lament requires a hopeful trust in God.

Trusting in More Than Our Own Faith: God's Resurrection of Hope

In the midst of my cancer journey, I've faced a temptation that is similar to Roth's, though it is not the same. My temptation is not to assert that God is not good, but rather I feel too weary and weak to trust that the new creation is coming. A hope and trust in God's promise is essential to maintaining a persistent prayer of lament and a life of compassionate protest in "this dark world" (Eph. 6:12 NIV)—protesting that this is not the way things are supposed to be. When a hopeful trust in God's promises is in short supply, it can feel like trying to run a race when you're short on oxygen: you slow down, you pant, you gasp for air. As strange as it sounds, the fact that the psalmist can bring anger, frustration, and protest to God is rooted in hope: if you don't hope that God is good and sovereign, you don't bother to bring your lament and thanksgiving to the Lord. Sometimes I feel too weak to hope, too tired and despairing to even lament.

When the word "cancer" is spoken by a doctor, it can feel like the sky has closed in—the world has become smaller, the background music to life has stopped.[33] In those moments, I was especially grateful for the presence and the prayers of brothers and sisters in the body of Christ offering laments and petitions on my behalf even when I felt too listless to pray these things myself. Yet even when others offer their care, it can feel like one is alone, a small little creature dwelling in dark silence. "I lie awake; I am like a lonely bird on the housetop" (Ps. 102:7). Yes, others care. But what will that matter if I'm dead in a few years? Yes, there can be treatment. But the treatment knocks me over like I've been hit on the head, and it won't make the cancer fully go away. It's stubborn and incurable.

But we face a similar stubbornness in other circumstances as well: the nurse discouraged by the stubbornness of childhood terminal illness; those working with people under the slavery of addiction; the Christian who prays for years that their loved one will come to faith in Christ. Why would God *not* respond to such prayerful petitions and the actions of witness that go along with them? Is the kingdom of Christ's peace really coming? How do we keep up the courage of asking, again and again, "Thy kingdom come"? Sometimes, I'm tired of "revolt," as Barth calls it. I'm tired of hoping.

And being on chemotherapy and steroids, I'm often just tired—in body and spirit. When I interact with people, I often feel resentment afterward because I felt like I poured out energy that I didn't have; I end up with a pounding headache and dizziness from the fatigue. Over twenty times I wrote about my deep "fatigue" on CarePages and asked for prayer for help from our God and Comforter: "In terms of chemo side effects, I continued to have new ones arise every few days, and the biggest challenge was sleep deprivation (and then fatigue) because of the steroids. . . . *Prayer request*: for a rhythm of rest and sleep in the Comforter." But at times, I was just tired of asking, tired of hoping.

There is hope—to keep lamenting, to keep acting in compassionate revolt and witness to the coming kingdom. But the hope is not in myself. I can't pull it off. I don't have the courage or persistence to do so on my own—to keep lamenting, to keep praising, to keep trusting. As a youth growing up in the church, I was often told to get "fired up" for Christ, go out and do great things for Jesus. There is something right about this—we are called not to apathy but to give up our life and energies for Christ, to act in protest and witness to the present and coming King. But this form of Christianity also cultivated a faith in my own faith—I sang "I have decided to follow Jesus" so many times that I was convinced that individual faith itself was the height of heroism.

90

In response to my CarePages, I've often received the response, "I admire your faith in the midst of this trial." I'm not really sure what this means—is faith something we deserve credit for, particularly if we are in a crisis? These responses sometimes implied that God didn't really deserve our faith in such circumstances—we're being gracious to God by heroically having faith in him when we face trials.

But I think the opposite is the case, particularly when we face the stubbornness of unanswered prayer and the stubbornness of a fallen world that won't seem to budge. I don't have faith in faith; I have faith in God and his promises. As Jesus says in John 3:3, "No one can see the kingdom of God without being born from above"—we can't even "see" the kingdom apart from the work of the Spirit. We don't deserve credit for this "seeing." We don't trust in our own sight of faith. We trust in God.

In times of doubt, I have often prayed this petition.

> The LORD will fulfill his purpose for me;
> your steadfast love, O LORD, endures forever.
> Do not forsake the work of your hands. (Ps. 138:8)

My hope and trust in God is not a human creation—it is the work of God's hands. Thus, I can bring it back to God and offer a lament: Where is your work in us, Lord, when hope seems gone? Will you fulfill your purpose for me when I feel too listless to hope in your coming kingdom? "Do not forsake the work of your hands." For I don't have confidence in my own hope. I have confidence that "he who began a good work in you will carry it on to completion until the day of Christ Jesus" (Phil. 1:6 NIV).

When the psalmist cries out for rescue, "O guard my life, and deliver me" (Ps. 25:20), the poet is not just "trying to revive hope" as an act of self-help—he calls to *God* for deliverance. In reflecting on this Psalm, John Calvin suggests we are to pray that God "would increase our hope when it is small, awaken it when it is dormant, confirm it when it is wavering, strengthen it when it is weak, and that he would even raise it up when it is overthrown."[34] We don't hope in hope. We hope

91

in a God who can make dry bones of hopelessness live again (Ezek. 37)—the God who raised Jesus Christ from the dead can surely resurrect my hope from the ashes, for we have something better to trust in than ourselves, better than our own heroic "faith." We have a God who does not forsake his work in us because it is, after all, *his* work and *his* covenantal promise to be our God.

6

Death in the Story of God and in the Church

Death comes to mind at the strangest times. In my life, I've been struck by thoughts of my own death and mortality at times when life seems most beautiful and precious. On my wedding day, amidst the joy and celebration of being united to my bride, thoughts of death and mortality also flashed through my mind. When my wife, Rachel, and I traveled in Ethiopia to meet our daughter, Neti, for the first time, the thought of my own death sunk into my stomach even as we delighted in her playful smile. When our son, Nathaniel, was delivered in the hospital room in Michigan, death and the frailty of human life struck me as well. None of these moments were morbid. But they were realistic, as if saying to me, "You are mortal, Todd; you are going to die." The creation is good—"the world is charged with the grandeur of God," to quote Gerard Manley Hopkins. Your wedding and hopes for a married life are good. The lives of your children and your hopes for their future are good. They are goods worth pouring out your life for. But your life is finite. You are going to die. You need to live as a mortal.

In these moments, the precious beauty of life and the prospect of death were experienced together. The incredible goodness of creation, including the hope in new life—in a marriage, in children, in creation as a whole—exposed me to what some philosophers and theologians have referred to as the "problem of good." I've reflected already in earlier chapters on the problem of evil. But there is a "problem" (if one does not believe in a good God) explaining the goodness in the world that goes far beyond the banal. "If the world is the chance assembly of accidental phenomena, why is there so much that we want to praise and celebrate? Why is there beauty, love, and laughter?"[1] God's creation is drenched with wonder and goodness: lush waterfalls and sandy deserts; children who can blow bubbles and wear crazy wigs; material bodies that can dance, play sports, and express sexual intimacy in the secure freedom of marriage. Who are you going to thank for it? If you have no one to thank, then you have not done justice to "the problem of good." The beauties and delights of creation point beyond themselves; they cry out to thank someone—a Creator. Indeed, apart from the specific philosophical "problem of good," Scripture indicates that God's creation is not just good—it's *very* good! "God saw everything that he had made, and indeed, it was very good" (Gen. 1:31). The psalmists often join the whole creation in giving praise to the Creator for the incredible gifts in creation.

> You have made the moon to mark the seasons;
>   the sun knows its time for setting.
> You make darkness, and it is night,
>   when all the animals of the forest come creeping out.
> The young lions roar for their prey,
>   seeking their food from God.
> When the sun rises, they withdraw
>   and lie down in their dens.
> People go out to their work
>   and to their labor until the evening.
>
> O Lord, how manifold are your works!
>   In wisdom you have made them all;
>   the earth is full of your creatures. (Ps. 104:19–24)

94

Creation itself is a theater of God's glory (to use a favorite metaphor of John Calvin). Every person has been "formed to be a spectator of the created world and given eyes that he might be led to its author by contemplating so beautiful a representation."[2] Beauty. Glory. Leading to thanksgiving to the Creator, the author and giver of all gifts.

The Prospect of Death and Our Life Stories

But why did I think of death so prominently on my wedding day and when I first held my children in my arms? I am not quite sure. In part I suspect that I was feeling the loss that comes with any gain. When I was single in my twenties, I would often wonder about my future—whom would I marry? Or would I marry at all? I could imagine different possibilities, and with each one, my life story would be different. While reading a novel or observing marriages around me, I could speculate about the pros and cons of marrying a particular type of person. An introvert or an extrovert? A Democrat, a Republican, or an Independent? There seemed to be no end to the possibilities. In certain ways, my life seemed to lie before me as an almost infinite set of possibilities.

But in receiving the gift of marriage to Rachel at our wedding, I was also making a commitment that reminded me of death. The vow is audacious: to take one's spouse "to have and to hold, from this day forward, for better, for worse, for richer, for poorer, in sickness and in health, until death do us part." This is it—until death parts us. No more speculation about other "possibilities." This particular, finite story is my one and only life story now—life with Rachel, married to Rachel. Likewise, although Rachel and I had spent years preparing for adoption—filling out an incredible amount of paperwork, getting piles of documents stamped and notarized—it wasn't until I first met Neti that it sunk in deeply: *this* is your daughter. This is who she is—and no other. She, along with Nathaniel, are distinct, particular persons. They are delightful children, bringing joy to Rachel and me and many others. But they also have the characteristics of all other people: they

95

are this and not that—their particularities are now a part of my life story in a way that will stick.

I will always be their father—that's who I am now. And yet . . . that word: "always." The permanence of commitment can seem presumptuous in light of the finitude of mortals and the frailty of life itself. "O LORD, what are human beings that you regard them, or mortals that you think of them? They are like a breath; their days are like a passing shadow" (Ps. 144:3–4). We are finite creatures, our lives are "like a breath." In the contemporary West, we often act as if we are self-made individuals, able to change the routes of our life story by putting a new search into Google and discovering our new self. If we get bored with the Christian faith, we could find a Buddhist website or get recommendations for a book on an innovative new religion on Amazon.com. If we want a new spouse, we could find "scientifically developed" recommendations for dating from the world of virtual reality. We could even leave our spouse and children to find a "new life" if we want—we've seen others do it, why not ourselves? All of these trends, it seems to me, are not only expressions of our alienation from God but, more specifically, expressions of our denial of death, of our creaturely finitude. Our story is not endless. Our story is not full of limitless possibilities. It has a shape—and we are not, in fact, the author of the story. We are finite creatures, not creators who know no limits. We live in the story, and while we can act in genuine freedom, we are not the master of a choose-your-own-adventure novel.[3]

With a cancer diagnosis, one's story seems to veer off the road of predictability and reasonable expectation. For my cancer, the causes are unknown, and the biggest risk factor is age: the median diagnosis age is thirty years older than my own, and only a tiny percentage of those diagnosed share my age and life stage. My diagnosis wasn't reasonable to "expect." But more than that, the prognosis disrupts the story line of where I expected death to come in. I recall spending a summer in high school with my aging grandparents on their farm in Kansas. As I interacted with them, I would wonder, *What will I be like in my seventies? Will I be bitter and regretful, or full of gratitude?* Even in my teens, I was anticipating much later parts of my story and trying to live in light of them.

None of us knows when we will die, but there are different kinds of "not knowing." Most of us don't have a "50 percent chance of living ten years" hanging over us—a number that is better than many cancer patients receive. I could live five years, ten years, or possibly even decades; who knows, besides God, the author of the story? But in the meantime, making sense of my own story can be a puzzle. Think for a moment: if you *knew* you were going to live just five more years, how would you live? Now imagine that instead, you *knew* you would live thirty years. Would the story line of how you live in the second scenario be different? I suspect it would be.

Of course, such thought experiments are artificial—none of us truly *knows* how long we will live. But seeing our present action in light of a life story is not optional. All of us—Christian or not—do this all the time, whether or not we realize it. In the words of Graham Swift's novel *Waterland*, "Only animals live entirely in the Here and Now. Only nature knows neither memory nor history. But man—let me offer you a definition—is the storytelling animal. Wherever he goes he wants to leave behind not a chaotic wake, not an empty space, but the comforting marker-buoys and trail-signs of stories." For "even in his last moments, it's said, in the split second of a fatal fall—or when he's about to drown—he sees, passing rapidly before him, the story of his whole life."[4]

With this passage from *Waterland*, I concur that we inevitably tell stories about our lives and live in light of larger narratives. But not all stories to live by are equally faithful and fruitful for God's kingdom. The story about my prognosis that I received from my doctor needs a supplement—indeed, more than that, it needs death and new life, by God's Spirit. As Christians, we confess that we live as actors in stories of which we are not the author; we enter into a narrative that comes from God through Scripture. The story is one in which God's creation is "very good." Yet it's also one that—precisely because of the God-given beauty and goodness of creation—calls forth our protest because things are not the way they are supposed to be in this "present evil age" (Gal. 1:4). To mourn and to protest is to testify that the gifts of creation are truly wondrous, that the communion with God and others that we taste in Christ is truly the way things are supposed to be—thus alienation and death are not truly "natural" but enemies of God and his kingdom. And these are not just abstract ideas. Our life stories need to be incorporated into the death and new life of Christ in community, where God's gifts of Word and sacrament are celebrated amidst birth and health, sickness and death. That community is the church. In one CarePages entry, as I prayed and hoped for a remission to come from the stem cell transplant, I reflected on the surprising gift that the church includes rather than represses dying and death in the story that it lives in—in God's story in Christ.

Death and Dying: A Surprising Gift of the Church?

"So, what have you been thinking about?" When I'm honest, high on my list in recent days has been death. . . .

Some of my thinking about death has the tone of lament, sadness, and loss. We are praying for a deep, long remission. I hope and pray for this. With the psalmist, I pray, "do not take me away at the midpoint of my life, you whose years endure throughout all generations" (102:24). Yet, as a mortal creature who doesn't know the future, I won't know *in advance* whether I will have a long remission. I will have tests every three to six months to see whether the cancer has returned, in the best-case scenario. This is a loss. But it's also a gift of sorts. All of us are mortal. But our Western culture is dominated by many forces that push us to deny the reality of death, to sequester the possibility and process of dying. It is an odd burden yet blessing of those who are in fields such as medical care, hospice work, and church ministry that they are given moments that can break through our culture's denial of dying and death. And I'm experiencing the new reality of that burden and gift—that I will have

98

frequent—very frequent—reminders of my mortality, no matter how long the remission lasts.

So, you're probably wondering, what in the world is the surprising gift of the church, the title of this section? During the last few weeks I led an adult Sunday school class in my local congregation on lament, providence, and life in Christ—some general and theological reflections from my cancer journey. In my church, we are blessed with children, young parents, people in their middle age, and people in their later years. In speaking to members of my congregation on this topic, it forced a level of honesty that I found striking: this is a place where funerals take place on a regular basis; in this room are cancer survivors who have gone through chemo; and there are others who have lost spouses and other loved ones to cancer and other diseases. The congregation is the only place (that I can think of!) in Western culture where we develop relationships, celebrate our faith and life together, and also extend those *same* relationships all the way through dying and death. A place of employment, a hospice—they have indispensable roles, but in neither is a community life that celebrates the birth of babies among the young and the old, and extends those same relationships all the way to death. It's a gift, really. It's a marvelous gift that the church who baptizes and celebrates new life in Christ also does funerals, mourns with the dying, and celebrates the promise of resurrection in Christ. For some young people, the church is one of the only places that they are exposed to death in a real, personal way—where someone they knew has died. And I think that is a gift of the church. I would go so far as to say that a top recommended question from me for "church shoppers" might be this: who would you like to bury you? Think about that one for a while!

Living as mortal creatures is part of living. Our bodies, like all that God has made, were created "very good" (Gen. 1:31) gifts from God. But as my body has recently been poked and prodded literally hundreds of times with injections, blood tests, IVs, and a catheter on

Monday, it reminds me that our bodies do not yet taste the fullness of the victory Christ has won. We live in hope, for the "last enemy to be destroyed is death" (1 Cor. 15:26). "When this perishable body puts on imperishability, and this mortal body puts on immortality, then the saying that is written will be fulfilled: 'Death has been swallowed up in victory.' 'Where, O death, is your victory? Where, O death, is your sting?'" (1 Cor. 15:54–55; Hosea 13:14 quoted).

For "Christ has been raised from the dead, the first fruits of those who have died" (1 Cor. 15:20). But Christ's victory over death is not grounds for us to pretend that we are not mortal, to push death and dying to the furthest corner of our minds. Rather, our hope in Christ can give us the courage to look members of our congregation in the face when we talk about our own death. By the Spirit, we've been united as brothers and sisters in Christ's body, such that "if one member suffers, all suffer together with it" (12:26). We can walk the path of life and the path of dying as one path because they share one hope: that in "body and soul, in life and in death," we belong to our "faithful Savior, Jesus Christ" (Heidelberg Catechism Q & A 1). While death is the final enemy to be defeated, it's a good thing that death and dying are included (rather than pushed to the margins) in the Christian story. Death and dying are included in the journey that congregations make together week by week, year by year, as testimony to their identity in Christ.

Death and dying are included—not excluded—in the story of God and the story of congregational life. Many today seek to overcome the shortcomings of the church, to improve its public relations and its popularity, to "reinvent" the church for a new day. The flaws in the church are deep and real. But in essence, the church is not the church because we believe in positive thinking, imagine a better world, or even because we believe in the importance of faith. The church is the church as a creature of God's Word—a creature that finds its life outside of itself, that does not have faith in faith so much as faith in the God of covenant promise made known in Christ. From one standpoint, the church is a gathering of sinners who are both old and young, healthy and sick, growing and dying. But, by God's promise, the church is also people who move through birth, health, dying, and even death on a journey to resurrection because they belong to Jesus Christ. For the end of the story of God, and of the church, is not death but resurrection. "Christ has been raised from the dead," and the defeat of death in resurrection comes through him and then to those who belong to him. "Christ the first fruits, then at his coming those who belong to Christ" (1 Cor. 15:20, 23).

Signs of Death and Signs of God's Promise

As I write this, my stomach is covered with bruises—blue, yellow, red, black. They come from injections that I have to give myself every twelve hours, and it's often difficult to find a part of my stomach that is clear enough from bruising to give another injection. I also receive a regular regimen of poison (chemo) to fight the out-of-control growth of cancer cells. Every time I go into the cancer lab, I am poked and prodded to discover where my cancer levels are. I have daily, bodily reminders of the current "reign of death." But thanks be to God, I live not only in the midst of the reign of death but also by hope in God's promise. This promise comes in the midst of bodily, human fellowship—in the church gathered for the Word preached, the Word in the water of baptism, and the Word in bread and wine. In all of these forms, God's promise challenges the finality of the reign of death for his people, who have become united to Christ. For "if we have died with Christ, we believe that we will also live with him. We know that Christ, being raised from the dead, will never die again; death no longer has dominion over him" (Rom. 6:8–9).

The signs of the current reign of death are not abstractions—they are sharp, bodily signs. As one who regularly receives those signs, I am grateful that the signs of God's promise, and God's new creation, are not abstractions either. Calvin is particularly insightful here. While some may think that our need for material, bodily signs of God's promise is merely for the sake of "illustration" for the dull-minded, Calvin insisted that our need for a material sign of God's promise is part of what it means to be a good, embodied creature. Therefore, even apart from our sin and alienation from God, we need material signs of God's life-giving presence and promise. In his comments on Genesis 2 and 3, Calvin interprets the tree of life as an external sign of God's promise by which God "stretches out his hand to us, because, without assistance, we cannot ascend to him. He intended, therefore, that man, as often as he tasted the fruit of that tree, should remember whence he received his life, in order that he might acknowledge that he lives not by his own power, but by the kindness of God alone." Thus, even before the fall, humanity needed material signs that could be seen, smelled, touched, and tasted, to "seal his grace to man."[5]

God's promise is far beyond an "abstraction" not only because it is received in a bodily, material way amidst other bodies—other persons in the body of Christ—but also because when God speaks, it is an *action*. God makes promises to his people as a covenantal God. "I will be their God and they will be my children" (Rev. 21:7; see also Exod. 6:7; Lev. 26:12). This is not just an observation that God makes. It is a promise, an action that brings us into a new state of affairs. In a similar way, when a minister said to Rachel and me at our wedding, "I pronounce you husband and wife," this was an *action*. New roles were conferred on us, new identities to live into—in the context of a community that would support and uphold these new identities. Likewise, God's covenantal promises, which are at the heart of the Psalms and at the heart of the hopes of God's people in Scripture, are not merely words or abstractions. Those who receive the covenantal promises are conferred a new identity. "Once you were not a people, but now you are God's people" (1 Pet. 2:10). Jesus Christ himself is the fulfillment and living enactment of God's promises. For "in him [Christ] every one of God's promises is a 'Yes'" (2 Cor. 1:20), and our identity is as those who are "in Christ," the covenant keeper and the covenant God in one. The Triune God is at the center of the action here—we *receive* forgiveness, new life, and a new communal context for our identity. For God's Word of promise is an action: it is *God* who works out his covenantal purposes through his Word, even as these purposes are worked out in and through us.

In God's promises, he pledges to adopt a people to be his own. In the New Testament, God's adoption of a people is sometimes considered a future reality. It is God's *promise* after all, and we have not reached the culmination of God's kingdom. Instead, we "groan inwardly while we wait for adoption, the redemption of our bodies" (Rom. 8:23). Yet our adoption is also a present reality, as Paul indicates a few verses earlier: for "all who are led by the Spirit of God are children of God. For you did not receive a spirit of slavery to fall back into fear, but you have received a spirit of adoption" (Rom. 8:14–15). We need God's Word in preaching, baptism, and the Lord's Supper as external signs of God's promise—that it *is* being fulfilled in the present but also that God's good creation will be renewed when the reign of sin and death is fully over, when the final kingdom comes. Through all of these signs, we taste covenantal fellowship with God and other Christians as ones who are dying yet who—through God's power—will move through death. In feeding on Christ in corporate worship, we encounter death again and again because by the Spirit, Christians die again and again as they taste the new creation that God will bring them into.

One of the ways the church bears witness to the place of death in God's story—over and against our death-denying culture—is in baptism. Baptism, of course, is not just about new life but unavoidably it is about death as well. "Do you not know that all of us who have been baptized into Christ Jesus were baptized into his death? Therefore we have been buried with him by baptism into death, so that, just as Christ was raised from the dead by the glory of the Father, so we too might walk in newness of life" (Rom. 6:3–4). In a sermon I heard at a baptism about a month after my diagnosis, the pastor said,

> Baptism is beautiful and good of course, but we don't get to walk away from the font without an honest acknowledgment of the brokenness of it all. There's something sad about baptism. Because implicit in it

103

is an acknowledgment that something went wrong, drastically wrong. We went wrong, horribly wrong. And God does not sit idly by and let it go. God did not turn a blind eye, God did not redefine the terms until everyone was fine. God dealt decisively with sin, evil, corruption, and wickedness.[6]

God decisively overcomes sin and death in his covenant fulfilled in the life, death, and resurrection of the covenant-in-person, Jesus Christ. But we live as God's baptized, covenantal people in hope—although God has dealt decisively with sin and death, we still live in their midst.

Death pokes and prods each time I go into the cancer clinic. And yet each time I celebrate baptism with my congregation, we celebrate the good news that the Spirit brings life, that the Spirit unites believers to Jesus Christ and his church and brings his people through death and into life in and through Christ. Likewise, in the Lord's Supper we celebrate the living presence of Jesus Christ, the Supper's host. But these gifts of new life in Christ are never without Christ's death—his death that is decisive for bringing sinners into God's covenant fellowship. And as we proclaim the all-sufficiency of Christ's death, we look toward the final banquet when God's kingdom has fully come. "For as often as you eat this bread and drink the cup, you proclaim the Lord's death until he comes" (1 Cor. 11:26). Through Christ's death, the God of the universe, who has life in himself, freely and graciously makes our ashes come alive, gathering scattered sinners who were "strangers and aliens" into membership in "the household of God" (Eph. 2:19). For "in Christ Jesus you who once were far off have been brought near by the blood of Christ" (Eph. 2:13). We will never move beyond the blood of Christ—for the final kingdom itself is a great, worshipful gathering of "singing with full voice, 'Worthy is the Lamb that was slaughtered to receive power and wealth and wisdom and might and honor and glory and blessing!'" (Rev. 5:12). Death will be defeated, but death is still a part of the drama of God's redemptive story that we participate in now as adopted children of God by the Spirit, coheirs with Christ—and part of the story that we will continue to sing about in the culmination of God's new creation.

The Denial of Death in Western Culture, and Death in the Church

In contrast to God's story, which includes and envelops death, the currents of our consumerist, Western culture move toward repressing dying and death. To come face-to-face with our mortality would be to encounter our frailty and limitations—showing the absurdity of our attempts to center the world on ourselves. But our consumerist culture would rather deny these limits. Western culture glorifies youth and spends billions of dollars annually to make the appearance of youth last longer and longer. The actual experience of dying and death is isolated to nursing homes, hospices, and the funeral industry, away from children and youth and the rest of the family. This cultural trend was exposed to me with particular potency while working in community development for six months in a rural area of Uganda. In that context, dying and death were thickly woven into everyday life. When I would meet a new family, I would often hear explanations like, "We have seven children, but only four are still living." Ailing and dying members of the "extended" family were not institutionalized but lived in the same house as children and young people. And death itself was an everyday thing—not a rare incursion. I remember writing about it at the time, saying death was like "enya," a staple food eaten at least twice a day. We should not romanticize this state of affairs in Uganda—this is not the way things are supposed to be. But we need to recognize that in the West today, we not only have better medical care but we also tend to put our elderly and sick out of sight. Intentionally or not, we isolate ourselves from the real-life dying and death of others, and we have a culture that is often so focused on positive self-esteem and accomplishing one personal "victory" after another that dying and death are pushed to the margins.

Our cultural moment provides an important opportunity for the Western church. Only in the church do we celebrate the new birth of a child the same day that we prayerfully walk with another through the valley of death. It's all in the same "space"—the space of the sanctuary with pulpit, font, and table—the space of the proclamation of God's promises culminated in the life, death, and resurrection of Christ, received by ear, by mouth, and on the skin. This is a "space" of the new creation—material signs of God's covenant promise. Like the psalms of lament, the space of pulpit, font, and table does not repress our current encounters with God's enemies, our current struggles with sin and death. But it brings them before the face of God so that Jesus Christ, the true King, exercises his lordship through Word and Spirit, conforming us to the image of the crucified servant, shaping us into children of the Prince of Peace.

Unfortunately, the Western church has often capitulated to our death-denying culture, missing its special calling as the one community that can weave into its fold not only birth and growth but dying and death as well. For example, in a growing trend, many funerals completely avoid the language of dying and death as well as the presence of the dead body—turning it all into a one-sided "celebration" of the life of the one who has died. In refusing to face the reality of death, we only attend to one side of the biblical paradox about death, forgetting that even the death of a very elderly person is not "altogether sweet and beautiful."[7] Jesus himself was "greatly disturbed in spirit and deeply moved" when he joined those who were mourning Lazarus's death, and he himself wept with them (John 11:33). Did Jesus weep because death was the final end for Lazarus? No—the Father gave Lazarus new life through Jesus's prayer, and his revived body became a walking parable for the new life that God brings. But Jesus still wept—even for one who would be raised again. And so should we.

But more than just the funeral, the loss of lament in corporate worship has coincided with a denial and suppression of death for many congregations. As Carl Trueman argues, corporate Christian worship "should provide us with a language that allows us to praise the God of resurrection while lamenting the suffering and agony that is our lot in a world alienated from its creator, and it should thereby sharpen our longing for the only answer to the one great challenge we must all face sooner or later. Only those who accept that they are going to die can

106

begin to look with any hope to the resurrection." The Psalms—with their laments, petitions, and praises—have been a staple of Christian worship for centuries. They, along with the sacraments of Christ's dying and new life, have incorporated death into the story of Christian worship. But the trend in much "modern worship" is "distraction and diversion" from death and dying. "Praise bands and songs of triumph seem designed in form and content to distract worshipers from life's more difficult realities."[8] However, as Pascal pointed out, "Distraction is the only thing that consoles us for miseries, and yet it is itself the greatest of our miseries."[9] Distraction from the stubborn realities of dying and death serves no one well—and it is particularly unhelpful for followers of the crucified Lord.

"Senseless" Dying and Death as Ones "Hidden with Christ in God"

One of the stubborn realities about death is that it often seems senseless. This is particularly clear with the death of a child, death through careless neglect, or death by an accident. But as I have seen a couple of my friends die from cancer since my diagnosis, their process of dying—of dramatically losing their body weight and moving deeper and deeper into pain while managing heavy painkillers—seemed absurd. It just doesn't seem like the right end to a life story. But I must admit that my own death is likely to appear the same way—the "end" of a life story that makes creation's gift twist and turn in breathless aches.

But the gospel is good news that is big enough to incorporate and envelop our dying and death, even when it seems senseless. After my diagnosis, I revisited a sermon manuscript from one of my favorite seminary professors. I heard the sermon in person sixteen years ago. Though I was fuzzy on the details, I remembered the power of his exposition of Colossians 3:1–4 about the surprising implications of being united to the resurrected Christ: "So if you have been raised with Christ, seek the things that are above, where Christ is, seated at the right hand of God. Set your minds on things that are above, not on things that are on earth, for you have died, and your life is hidden with Christ in God. When Christ who is your life is revealed, then you also will be revealed with him in glory."

So, having been united to the resurrected Christ, should we expect our lives to be one "victory" after another, becoming increasingly immune to the sufferings of the world? Not for Paul, as my professor, John L. Thompson, noted. Alongside this passage in Colossians, he preached on the death of Jephthah's daughter, a death that appears nonsensical and absurd if there ever was one: she was killed because of a rash vow made by her father (Judg. 11:29–31). Yet Thompson noted that the early church father Origen considered her a "martyr" whose apparently senseless death contributed to the defeat of evil.[10] This was not a "throwaway" comment. Origen's own father and many of his closest friends were martyred. He knew that such deaths look senseless—they look like godforsakenness. From Origen's earthly perspective, the death of Jephthah's daughter and martyrs around him look like defeats. But in Christ, as Paul says, "your life is hidden with Christ in God." Its true glory is hidden from view, to be later "revealed with him in glory." But right now it is hidden, safely hidden, "with Christ in God."

"What Origen has been saying is in many ways what Martin Luther meant by the theology of the cross," Thompson notes. "Namely, that the Christian life looks a lot more like humiliation and rejection than it does like triumph and glory." For Origen, the martyrs "lived their lives in faith and faithfulness, even when neither life nor God seemed kind to them. Even through the cruelest ambiguity, when their faithful discipleship bore no visible fruit, they still kept the faith. And they kept the faith, I think, because however much they suffered, however unlikely it *seemed* that God was with them, they still trusted that their lives were safe—hidden with Christ."

Thompson admonished his listeners that when their lives take turns that appear to be dead ends, they should remember that they are "hidden with Christ in God." Then came a line I had forgotten: "Remember that, please, when you're only in your thirties or forties, or your fifties or sixties, and the doctor says it may not be benign."[11]

In tears, I heard this sermon in a way unlike how I had heard it sixteen years earlier. The deaths of my friends with cancer and my own death will likely *appear* to be absurd: an abrupt and seemingly arbitrary end to a life with so many strands, so many joys from God's good creation, so many stories longing for completion. But as Thompson went on to point out, "While all this may sound somber," there is "good news" here in the promise that our lives are hidden with Christ in God. "It's not your job to fashion your own success as if you were God. It's not your job to write the last chapter of your life. It's not your job to tie up the loose ends. It's not your job to make sense of everything. Your life is hid with Christ in God: Let it be your highest act of faith and faithfulness to leave it there! Leave the ambiguity of discipleship at the cross. Let God gather up the fragments. Let God finish the story."[12]

7

Praying for Healing and Praying for the Kingdom

Silence. I wondered whether I had said something wrong. I was sitting in a Western Theological Seminary classroom with a group of students and faculty; we were planning a worship service for the seminary community to pray for me shortly before the stem cell transplant. Some wanted to call it a "healing service." Others wanted to emphasize a service of "sending and lament"—I would be sent to the hospital for a month and then be in isolation from public places for several months. I would receive high doses of a poison that would lead to death if it were not for a rescue plan (the transplant), as the next chapter will explore. So, should we lament or pray for healing? Or should we do both?

When a student suggested that we not only have prayers for healing but prayers for lament as well, I agreed. But before the silence, I went a bit further. "I am deeply appreciative of all of the prayers that I've received. But I would prefer that public prayers offered on my behalf would be for 'deep remission'—rather than a 'cure,' in the sense of setting back the clock to a time before my diagnosis." At this point, I had already received numerous prayers for a cure, often with verses like Matthew

18:19 quoted: "If two of you agree on earth about anything you ask, it will be done for you by my Father in heaven." The prayers for my healing were passionate and persistent from the seminary, churches, family, and friends. I was grateful for these prayers—for all of the prayers. In prayer, we can freely pour out our hearts to God, and God himself is the primary audience. I didn't want to be the "prayer police"—our feeble prayers are not just our own; we pray through the Holy Spirit in Jesus Christ, who completes and perfects our prayers as the great High Priest.

Yet, God does give us biblical patterns and a Christ-shaped path for our prayers to follow. There are better and worse ways to pray, and this is particularly apparent when we pray for someone in their presence. Sometimes the spontaneous prayers for me seemed to point more to the ones praying than to God. And at times the spontaneous prayers left me feeling alienated and misunderstood. Ultimately, our prayers for a Christian brother or sister should reflect and enter into our common identity in Christ—sharing in their suffering, praying laments and petitions with the psalmists, and praying our Lord's Prayer that Christ's cross-shaped kingdom would come. Whether or not we use the words of the psalmists and the Lord's Prayer in our spontaneous prayer, these God-given prayers—in light of the canon of Holy Scripture—illuminate what it means to pray as ones who belong to Jesus Christ, the High Priest. At times, those around me wanted to jump to the healing prayer while bypassing the lament that went along with it—as if Jesus should have skipped his weeping with the family of Lazarus over their loss before he brought healing and restoration to Lazarus and his family: "When Jesus saw her [Mary] weeping, and the Jews who came with her also weeping, he was greatly disturbed in spirit and deeply moved" (John 11:33). Sometimes we want to skip over the messy part of joining Christ in lament to get to our prayers for healing. Yet whether we are asking for prayers for ourselves or praying for others in need, we need to follow the pattern of the psalmists, embodied in Christ: both lament and petition are brought before the covenant Lord.

But why the awkward silence in this worship-planning meeting? Was I, the theology professor, undercutting the power of petitionary prayer when I said I'd prefer not to receive prayers for a "total cure" that turned back the clock to before my diagnosis? Was I choosing a lamenting Jesus *rather than* one who heals? In the meeting itself, I said I just didn't know what a "total cure" would mean. God can and does heal—I had seen God work through healing both in the church in the United States and in my time of mission work in East Africa. But in this case, a loss was inevitable—an ongoing loss was already underway.

Did I believe that God could bring complete healing, even to an incurable cancer? Yes—in the sense that it would not be beyond God's power. With Jeremiah the prophet, we can pray to the Lord that "it is you who made the heavens and the earth by your great power and by your outstretched arm! Nothing is too hard for you" (32:17). But praying for healing for someone with a cancer like this is a little like praying for healing for someone who has lost a limb. God can provide healing. But it will be a different order of healing. Until the final restoration in the resurrection, prayers of healing in circumstances like this need to be paired with prayers of ongoing lament, because nothing will turn back the clock. Even if my cancer completely disappeared—and I had no detectable levels left—doctors would *expect* the cancer to return. Thus even if I was miraculously and immediately cured, I would need to continue on maintenance chemotherapy for the rest of my life, along with cancer tests every three to six months. There would still be a deep loss. Consequently, if I were to pray that things would become like they were before my diagnosis, it would simply be an act of denial. Whether God provided healing now, over a long period of time, or in final glory, there is no question that we can and should pray for healing. But not without lament.

In the previous chapters, I have been reflecting on the intersection of the story of God in Christ with the shock and surprise of my cancer diagnosis and its implications through the course of my early treatment. Each chapter has given different angles into that part of the cancer story in light of God's story in Christ. This chapter and the final two move on to consider the second and third stages of my cancer story: when I was admitted into the hospital for a stem cell transplant, and then my time of recovery after the transplant. In particular, this chapter and the next have CarePages entries that I wrote while I was in the hospital. Through these chapters, I reflect on how my cancer story (in these later stages) continues to intersect with the weightier story of God in Christ. This chapter focuses on questions that arose in the seminary meeting (described above) that I continued to explore while I was hospitalized: How should we pray for healing? What does it mean to faithfully pray as a community of Christians for someone with a cancer with no known cure? Moreover, what does it mean to bring petitions to God as followers of Jesus Christ and the path of his cross, praying for his kingdom to come on earth?

Prayers for Healing, "Quick Fixes," and the Body

Sometimes Christians assume that prayer for healing needs to take place on our timetable—that if it's really *God* who brings healing, it should be an immediate, "shock and awe" experience. But God is free to heal in his own time—even when the timing does not make sense to us. After my diagnosis, a friend of mine shared about the shape of answered prayer in his life in overcoming a speech impediment. The impediment was not only deeply embarrassing (like King George VI's in the film *The King's Speech*) but also seemed to be a roadblock to his growing calling to become a preacher of God's Word. Yet one evening while he was in college, he went to bed with the confidence that his speech impediment would disappear the next day. He had received therapy for the impediment for ten years, but now—*finally*—he was going to experience relief. Why? Because he was going to attend a healing service, and he had been told that if he had the faith that God would heal, then God would do so. My friend attended the service and received healing prayers with confidence that God would take away this impediment. But he was not healed. The impediment continued.

However, that was not the end of the story. Over the course of the next several years, through many, many hours of continued exercises and therapy, healing gradually came. My friend gives God thanks for

114

answering his prayer, but many Christians don't know how to respond to his story. If God were going to heal, why didn't God just do it immediately, apart from the many hours of therapy?

What these Christians miss is that every breath we have is a gracious gift from God—we are completely, utterly dependent on the Creator. Whenever healing comes, God deserves praise. God is free to heal quickly or over a long process, and surprise at the long path to my friend's answer to prayer seems to assume that God doesn't work through material means like bodies and the often arduous physical work that it takes for bodies to move toward healing. God is "above" that. On the one hand, I think we *should* pray for our physical needs rather than just assuming that God is only concerned about "the soul." We should pray not just about "spiritual" things but for our physical well-being as well. In praying that God provides for our daily bread in the Lord's Prayer, we ask (in the words of the Heidelberg Catechism), "Do take care of all our physical needs so that we come to know that you are the only source of everything good."[1] Whatever good health we have comes from the bounty of God, the fountain of all goodness; we should petition and give thanks.

But like the answered prayer of my friend, God's healing of the body is frequently a long road that does not bypass the processes of the body itself. Indeed, some of our bodily wounds may not be healed until we pass from this life into the next as sharers in the glory of the resurrected Christ. Thirteen years ago, I suddenly started to experience severe back pain. There was no inciting incident, but the pain was very real and constant. However, I still looked like a healthy, active man in his twenties. Seeing this, my first physical therapist tried a "quick fix"—pounding on a knotted muscle. Immediately after trying this, she had to bring me straight to the emergency room—I was in much worse shape than she realized. Likewise, I received many prayers for my back and my cancer that have desired a "quick fix." They prayed that my back pain would immediately vanish . . . and years later others prayed that I would be immediately "cured" of my incurable cancer. At times, I just appreciate the prayer and the charitable intentions behind it. But sometimes, similar to the experience of many people with a long-term disability, I get tired of the impatience of these prayers—an impatience that seems to diminish the material, embodied nature of my life as a creature, my life as one who has been united to the resurrected Christ but is *still groaning* for the new creation.

As I write this, I still have daily, chronic back pain. I don't know "why" I haven't been fully healed. That's an open question. But I do not doubt that God has been active through the journey of the last thirteen years and that God will heal in the end. In the journey of the last thirteen years, I have had some recovery from my back pain, and I give thanks to God for the renewed health and strength. But it has come inch by inch, with hundreds of hours of therapy, exercise, and stretching. Along the road, I've come to live with my finite, bodily limitations, even as I groan and ask God for more healing. In the midst of it, I've been forced to face my own tendency to ignore my body's warning signs and needs; I've had to face the fact that I hate asking others for help—even though I cannot lift more than a small weight without having sharp pain. On an experiential level, this long road of both healing and continued physical pain has forced me to acknowledge on a daily basis that I am an embodied, dependent creature. Each measure of healing and each continued breath is a gift from the gracious Creator.

In a similar way, even if God were to provide a "quick fix" to my cancer, I would still have a long road ahead—with maintenance chemotherapy, frequent cancer tests, and so on. God is active. God graciously gives gifts of healing and strength to my finite, aching body. But impatient prayers for an "immediate cure" seem to tread on my loss rather than bring it in lament, petition, and thanksgiving before the Lord.

Petitions, Heroic Prayers, and Going Bald

In addition, sometimes these "quick fix" instincts seem to reflect what Luther calls "a theology of glory" rather than "a theology of the cross." "Glory" here refers not to an expectation of our final glorious union with the resurrected Christ, but to the way in which we capitulate to theologies that *glorify ourselves* rather than the crucified and risen Christ. As Gerhard Forde notes about the distinction in Luther's thought, "A theology of glory always leaves the will in control," rather than a theology of the cross in which we die and live in and through the crucified Lord.[2] Recently I read about a Christian family who went to their pastor after they had a child born with autism. After "unsuccessful" prayers for healing, the pastor asked that they search their hearts for "unconfessed sin."[3] Was this pastor really praying for Christ's cross-shaped kingdom to come, or did he just think that Christians should have lives that are more convenient and carefree than one devoted to caring for someone with a disability? Clearly, he saw prayer as a kind of bargain—we do our part (taking care of unconfessed sin) and then God does his part (healing). Ultimately, our own will is in control, in this view, since God's fulfillment of the bargain should be predictable. But as we know from Job, and even more so from Jesus, living a righteous life does not make one immune to great suffering. God is not our debtor. God does not owe us a long life of convenience and upward mobility, as characterized by the American dream. Biblical petitions hinge on God's promises, not on our own will's self-glorification rooted in its sense of entitlement or self-pity.

At times, I received prayers that seemed to make the one praying the hero of the prayer—as if the "prayer warriors" were the primary actors in prayer, with God filling an ancillary role. I recall one card that I received with a poem about there being no power on earth "greater" than the power of prayer. But the eloquent poem made no mention of God. Ouch. Do we believe in God or in the "power of prayer"?

Approaches to prayer like this seem to assume that God is asleep at the wheel until we wake him up. Charitably framed, perhaps their prayers were a form of lament and petition, like the disciples who woke up Jesus on the boat because he appeared to be asleep on the job. But are the disciples the true heroes of the drama for their act of waking Jesus—or was it Jesus, who commanded the winds and the waves (Mark 4:31–35)? Sometimes we let ourselves be overtaken by fear because we assume that we are the heroes of prayer and that God will be irresponsible if we don't do "our job." What were we to think, for example, when I had an unexpected hospital visit because of my sharp pain and I was *not* able to contact people to request prayer? Some seemed to fear that I would be left in quite bad hands without having "prayer warriors" engaged.

These attitudes sometimes emerge from the misunderstanding of a common parable that Jesus told about prayer in Luke 18:1–8. In the parable, a persistent widow continually brings her plea to an unjust judge until he gives in and gives her justice. So the point of the parable is that we should (and need to) be persistent like the widow if we want our prayers answered, right? No. In the parable the unjust judge is not God. God is not an unjust judge who hears us only with an army of widows on our side. "And will not God grant justice to his chosen ones who cry to him day and night? Will he delay long in helping them? I tell you, he will quickly grant justice to them" (vv. 7–8). Luke says that Jesus tells this parable about the "need to pray always and not to lose heart" (v. 1). The perseverance of the widow in her requests is commendable—for sometimes heaven can seem silent, and God can *seem* like an unjust judge. But the punch line in the parable for why we should "not lose heart" in praying always is that God is *not* asleep at the wheel until we wake him up—God is good and gracious and always on time in providing for his covenantal children.[4]

Yet at times our prayers fail to point to God as the generous source of all good. We sometimes pray on a path of self-glorification rather than participation in the way of the cross in Jesus Christ. I am not immune—I have prayed along this path that reflects a "theology of glory" as well. It is for good reason that our Lord includes a prayer of confession and forgiveness of others in his prayer for us: "forgive us our debts, as we also have forgiven our debtors. And do not bring us to the time of trial, but rescue us from the evil one" (Matt. 6:12–13). Although prayer is an act of obedience, we still sin as we pray. Even as we pray and receive prayer from others, we need to receive and give forgiveness; we need deliverance from trial and the evil one, even in the act of praying.

However, in my time of cancer treatment, I have also received prayers—at the Western Theological Seminary prayer service, for example—that were on the path of pilgrimage toward our Lord. They were prayed with both tears of lament and joy (with the psalmist), and they communally prayed our common prayer as disciples of Christ: Thy kingdom come, Thy will be done, for God alone provides deliverance. The petitions moved along the path of the Lord's Prayer, shaping us into a people conformed to Christ and the way of the cross in him. A week after the Western Seminary chapel, the seminary community gathered again while I was in the hospital for what came to be called the "Bald Guy Challenge." I wrote about it afterward in my CarePages.

The high-dose chemo that I receive before the transplant will lead to the loss of my hair. Since it can be disconcerting to have clumps of one's hair fall out, it was recommended that I shave my head before things got started. I did so—but I was not alone!

Sixteen others from Western Theological Seminary joined me, acting in prayerful solidarity. It was coordinated with a fund-raiser for the Multiple Myeloma Research Foundation (MMRF), a very significant nonprofit organization that researches new treatments for my form of cancer. In the end, I was joined in head shaving by the president of Western Seminary, Timothy Brown, four other professors, several staff, and numerous students—including one female student at the seminary. The event took place on February 22 while I was in Butterworth Hospital, but I was present on a big-screen television via Skype. My nurses gathered around the screen—it was a fun and funny event, filled with joy. And in the end, it raised over $3,000 for the MMRF.

As I said in a note to the volunteers, you didn't have to lose your hair. You did it out of love in Christ. Thank you for that—I feel less lonely when I look in the mirror and I'm surprised by what I see! ("If one member [of the body of Christ] suffers, all suffer together with it" [1 Cor. 12:26].)

In addition, some students set up a gathering for prayer during the times that I would receive high-dose chemo while I was at the hospital. Some might frame such a meeting as a way to keep me "covered" in prayer—a phrase that I've often found ambiguous. Is it implying that God is an unjust judge, ungracious and begrudging, who wouldn't be paying attention if I wasn't "covered" in prayer? Yet when I heard of student gatherings like this one, I was grateful—I sensed they were acts of solidarity in and with the body of Christ as I was having poisons infused into my body. They were joining me in lament, joining me in petition—suffering with the one who suffers, bringing all of our burdens to our loving, covenant Lord. They were praying in and through Christ the Head who gathers and perfects his people's feeble petitions by the Spirit's power.

An Unexpected Hospital Stay, and "Data" in Prayer Requests

Four days after the prayer service for me at the seminary, I unexpectedly entered the hospital. I had received some preparatory chemo, and my white counts dropped to nearly zero. But what made it dangerous was my very high fever. I alternated between times of trying to manage quite severe pain and fatigue and times of mental alertness. My mind moved again and again to prayer, not only to pray myself but to reflect on what prayer itself is. I was in isolation because of my depressed immune system, but whenever I had a phone call or an email, there was an immediate question for an "update" and a list of "prayer requests." While these questions arose from genuine concern, at times it felt like people wanted the "data" of what to pray for because God might be slacking off and they needed to remind him of the specifics. Five days into my hospital time, I put some of my thoughts regarding prayer into a CarePages entry.

Petition and Communion with God

I love the book of Psalms. It contains many petitions: crying out to God in need, asking God to hear our cries to display his covenant love even when it doesn't look like we're being loved (i.e., we're in a mess). But imagine what the book of Psalms would be like if it were just a long list of specific things we want from God: "Oh God, please help Ethan's white counts go up" or something like that. Now, I'm not complaining about prayers being specific—I ask and continue to ask for prayers for my own white counts to go up. But what is amazing about the Psalms is that it's all set in the context of Israel's wondrous covenant-making God. The psalmist does not just speak the word "praise" to God; the psalmist "will tell of all your wonderful deeds" (Ps. 9:1). Creation, God's covenant with Abraham, Sinai, the exodus . . . the drama of God's mighty acts are recalled again and again; the list of God's mighty deeds is celebrated. And as Christian readers, God's mighty acts of power and love culminate in Jesus Christ. Praying with the psalmist means praying in a context where we are addressing a quite specific God, entering into communion with him in our cries of praise, confession, and lament, and are simultaneously united in communion with others who have been united together in Christ by the Spirit. So prayers of petition are good—no, they are absolutely necessary. But praying as Christians with the psalmist, these prayers should occur amid divine-human communion *and* human-human communion at the same time.

Avoiding Unintentional Mechanizing and Dehumanizing in Praying Together

What am I trying to avoid by resisting a "list of data" approach to sharing prayer requests? I'm afraid that a list of medical updates tends to individualize and mechanize the prayer process. Rather than praying in the context of sharing mutual burdens and joys, we bring "information" to God ("please raise Todd's blood counts") and hope that it "works" in giving an answer. Now don't mishear me. I think it's wonderful to pray some version of that prayer. But if our petitions are focused on just receiving a specific outcome rather than being part of our ongoing communion with God and each other, it can turn prayer into a kind of slot machine or "answer machine." We should petition and plead for God to answer our prayer, but in a very real sense, the "point" of prayer is as an aspect of our broader life with God and with one another, not just to get what we want from a specific wish list.

Second, a "list of data" approach can tend to define the person being prayed for by those numbers or data and thus unintentionally dehumanize them; even in the darkest moment of their struggle, they are people who laugh, make fun of themselves, enjoy (or hate) their latest meal, wonder about the future, and reflect on the past. They are not defined by a one-colored, sadness- or hope-laden lens, even when they endure some really nasty bone pain or experience a really terrible loss in relationship or of another sort.

Yesterday morning, in the midst of my bone pain, I noted to my new nurse that her patient not only has a doctorate but was watching PBS cartoons during his breakfast time. (What a great episode of *Curious George*!) Also, in one of the prayer updates, I noted that one of my moments of greatest delight this week was that for a whole *hour* on Tuesday, I felt alert enough to read from a long, nerdy book about the Trinity and providence. (Pleasure reading, of course! One nurse said I needed a head examination.) For me, there is something humanizing about these interactions as I tie some of them into my "cancer journey." I don't want to be seen *just* as the "cancer guy" or "the need" in the body of Christ but as someone who is facing a tremendous struggle yet also has so many unexpected and undeserved blessings, someone who really enjoyed the chicken tenders at lunch (I was rejoicing about hospital food today!), someone who likes to make silly jokes to his three-year-old daughter, someone who is really glad that most other people aren't as much of a nerd as he is. Cancer does not define me. Ultimately, my life and identity in Christ define me. I am a quirky, sometimes silly, sometimes (OK, often) serious person who has been saved from his sin by Christ's cross, united to Christ by the Spirit to live as one of God's adopted children.

OK, my strength is reaching its limit. But a final caveat: please do not feel "accused" if your prayers are often "data only" prayers.

122

I describe it so well because I have done it and continue to do it so often. I'm speaking to myself! But I'm also giving a rationale for why, when possible, I plan to continue to frame our praying together in terms of communion with God, even as I also give the data/information for our update. For we are "hidden with Christ in God" (Col. 3:3), praying as ones who enjoy communion with the Triune God in a profound way.

Petitions, Healing, and Faith

Prayer is a divinely ordained means of living in fellowship with God and each other. We pray in response to God's Word of promise—the promise to be our God, which is an action that brings us into God's story as characters in God's drama. Thus, we pray "our Father" as ones whom the Spirit has united to Christ, as adopted children of the covenant. We cannot understand biblical statements about prayer as petition apart from this context, centered in the promise of God's lovingkindness so central to the Psalms and embodied in Jesus Christ, the Messiah, the covenant-in-person.

Yet although prayer is a mode of communion with God and other adopted children in Christ, it still *asks*, it petitions.[5] When Jesus says to "pray then in this way," his model for prayer is not one of introspective preoccupation. It turns the focus to God and his kingdom, making petition upon petition. He asks for God's name to be made holy, his kingdom to come and his will to be done, and follows this with a list of imperatives, asking God to be the actor: "Give us. . . ." "Forgive us. . . ." "Lead us. . . ." "Deliver us. . . ." Jesus commands us to petition—to ask in the context of our covenantal adoption.

But how are we to fit together the commands to petition with the prayer for God's will to be done? Both are contained in the Lord's Prayer, but the potential tension becomes even clearer when we look at other passages about the teaching of Christ on prayer in the Gospels. On the one hand, "Thy kingdom come, Thy will be done" is a prayer of relinquishment of our own way—a prayerful alignment of the human will to God's own will. As Jesus prayed in the garden of Gethsemane, "My Father, if it is possible, let this cup pass from me; yet not what I want but what you want" (Matt. 26:39). On the other hand, earlier in Matthew's Gospel, Jesus says, "If two of you agree on earth about anything you ask, it will be done for you by my Father in heaven" (Matt. 18:19); and "Whatever you ask for in prayer with faith, you will receive" (Matt. 21:22; see also Mark 11:23–24). Those phrases can be encouraging or haunting: "anything you ask"; "whatever you ask." Taken as abstract propositions about prayer, they seem to fly in the face of Jesus's own prayer in the garden—"let this cup pass from me." The Father did not grant his petition. As C. S. Lewis writes, the second set of passages seems to require not just a faith in God that is conditional on God's will but "faith that the particular thing the petitioner asks will be given him. It is as if God demanded of us a faith which the Son of God in Gethsemane did not possess, and which if He had possessed it, would have been erroneous."[6]

As I read Lewis's essay in my hospital bed, the issue was not a mere abstraction. If Jesus teaches us to *ask* in prayer, and God is the Creator and Sustainer, then as Augustine says, God is "the all-powerful Doctor." Unlike human doctors, "God made your body. God made your soul. God knows how to re-create whatever He created. He knows how to re-form what he Himself formed."[7] God is good and powerful and able to heal. Even if I would still have a long road of testing and maintenance ahead, healing even multiple myeloma is certainly not beyond God's power. Likewise, God is good and powerful and able to deliver Christ from "the cup" of suffering on Calvary. Jesus commands us to *ask* in his model prayer and says that "whatever you ask" in prayer with faith will be answered; yet, anticipating the suffering of Calvary, Jesus *asked* for another way but did not have his petition granted. How are we to offer our petitions in light of this apparent tension about prayer in the life and teaching of Jesus himself?

While Lewis's essay vividly portrays the possible tension, we have to ask whether this is a biblically derived paradox or whether we've misinterpreted passages in order to make the contrast so sharp. "Whatever you ask for in prayer with faith, you will receive" (Matt. 21:22). Should we reason *retroactively* from passages like Matthew 21:22, such that if one *does not* receive a positive answer to prayer, it is due to a lack of faith? We've seen a parallel temptation to this before in the mechanistic reasoning of the "friends" of Job. Job both lamented and petitioned in his suffering; the book tells us that Job's suffering was *not* due to Job's sin or a deficiency in his devotion to God. He "was blameless and upright, one who feared God and turned away from evil" (Job 1:1). The Lord soundly rebukes Job's friends for their retroactive reasoning that puts the fault on Job's lack of devotion, for they "have not spoken of me what is right, as my servant Job has" (42:7).

In the Gospels, Jesus is not contradicting this earlier biblical teaching in the book of Job. Jesus often brings healing as a sign of the kingdom that has come in his person. Indeed, Jesus responds even to "outsiders" such as gentiles who seek him out in faith.[8] Trust in Jesus is a sufficient condition for the petition to be heard by God. And when Jesus freely responds by healing the petitioner, it is "evidence that the kingdom of God is being inaugurated here and now by Jesus as the agent of divine mercy (Mark 6:53–56; Matt. 14:34–36)."[9] Yet, like the book of Job, the Gospels do not support retroactive reasoning that would lead us to think that the suffering who have *not* received healing are at fault from sin or a lack of faith. As biblical scholar David Crump argues, "The gospel writers carefully insist that *faith itself is not the cause of miracles.*"[10] Many of Jesus's miracles are performed "*in spite of* the disciples' *lack of faith*," and others are performed "quite independently of any apparent faith."[11] Rather than faith causing the miracles themselves, the miracles of Jesus are used as vivid signs and testimonies to God's power and presence in Jesus, the Messiah. These testimonies call onlookers to faith—though like his parables, they are instruments in leading some to faith, while others turn away in light of these miraculous signs.[12] While the Gospels indicate that nothing more than faith in Christ is necessary to present a petition to the God of deliverance, they give us no formula indicating that asking in faith will make God bring healing.

In addition, Lewis's tension is put in a new light when the passages about asking for "anything" by faith are received in the context of Jesus and his mission in the Gospels rather than as abstract propositions.[13] As Donald Hagner notes about the "whatever you ask for in prayer" passage in Matthew, "Jesus does not offer his disciples magical power to do whatever they please or to perform extraordinary feats for their own sake. . . . All must be related to the purpose of God that is in the process of being realized."[14] We are invited to ask for "anything"—but in the context of praying for God's will to be done, for God's kingdom to come.

Petitioning and Aligning with God's Will: Christ's Prayer at Gethsemane

Yet these exegetical explanations still leave open a raw existential question: given that we are to *ask* according to God's purpose and will, how could it *not* be the will of God to heal one of his suffering children? God can do it. Why doesn't he always heal? During my time on chemo, I joined many others in praying for the healing of a six-year-old child in a devout Christian family from his cancer. He died. How could this young child's healing *not* be God's purpose and will?

Again, we must return to the luminous mystery of Christ at Gethsemane. At Gethsemane, Christ prays for the cup of suffering to pass, yet he submits to the Father's will and purpose rather than his own desire to escape the cross. At Gethsemane, we see the Lord's Prayer in action: "Gethsemane suggests the deepest meanings of the prayer: 'Do not let us be led into the Testing, but deliver us from evil.'"[15] Jesus asked to be led from the time of trial, to be delivered from evil. Yet the petition of the one who defines perfect faith—"Jesus the pioneer and perfecter of our faith" (Heb. 12:2)—was not granted. His cup of suffering was not taken away. Indeed, "Jesus offered up prayers and supplications, with loud cries and tears, to the one who was able to save him from death" (Heb. 5:7). God was *able* to save Jesus from death on a cross at Golgotha. But God did not do it. "The scene [at Gethsemane] is

126

terrible, not because Jesus must suffer, but because his suffering is the will of the God who is powerful enough to prevent it."[16] The problem is not God's lack of power, nor a deficiency in God's love. The denial of Jesus's petition does not arise from a failure to ask for another way than the cross or a lack of faith in the God of power and love. Jesus presents his heart to the Father in Gethsemane as a way to bring his will into alignment with the God of power and love who wills and works in mysterious, hidden ways: through the cross.

Praying in the Way of the Cross

When we come to God thinking that we are the heroes of prayer, we have forgotten the cross of Christ. When we assume that God only wills healing and joy rather than suffering in our lives now, we have forgotten the cross of Christ. When we act as if life with the resurrected Christ should be just one victory upon another, we have forgotten the cross of Christ. For while the death of Christ was a once for all sacrifice, ambassadors of the gospel do not skip over the cross to experience "resurrection living." In the words of Paul, "We proclaim Christ crucified, a stumbling block to Jews and foolishness to Gentiles" for "God chose what is foolish in the world to shame the wise; God chose what is weak in the world to shame the strong; God chose what is low and despised in the world, things that are not, to reduce to nothing things that are, so that no one might boast in the presence of God" (1 Cor. 1:23, 27–29). At the center of God's revelation is not a secret about how to live a happier, healthier life, or a message that God's work is transparent to our eyes in a steady, upward journey. Those united to Christ by the Spirit follow the way of the crucified Lord, which does not seek out suffering for its own sake but recognizes that God both acts and hides in the most unlikely places. In Luther's words, "He who does not know Christ does not know God hidden in suffering. Therefore he prefers works to suffering, glow to the cross, strength to weakness, wisdom to folly."[17]

We live in an age that wants a Christian life filled with the "glow" of an improved life. I recently noticed in a bookstore that most of the

Christian books were classified in the "self-help" section, and when I looked at the books that were there, I couldn't really disagree with the classification. But this is not the message of "Christ crucified." We can open our hearts before our loving Father in prayer, but as we pray, we pray on a path toward a particular end: "Thy will be done," like our Lord did in the garden. In prayer, we need to be on a path of asking for God's kingdom to come, allowing our desires for a glowing and tidy middle-class life to be put on the cross.

After writing about the theology of the cross in his first letter to the Corinthians, Paul returns to the theme in his second letter when he has to explain why his life does not look like one victory upon another. Paul's own petition for release from the thorn in his flesh was not granted—he was not healed or delivered. "I appealed to the Lord about this, that it would leave me, but he said to me, 'My grace is sufficient for you, for power is made perfect in weakness.' So, I will boast all the more gladly of my weaknesses, so that the power of Christ may dwell in me" (2 Cor. 12:8–9). Paul's petition to God was not denied because of a lack of faith. In the mystery of the God who works mightily in the weakness of the cross, his request was heard by God, but God put Paul back onto a cross-shaped path. In the midst of that cruciform path, Paul was convinced that the power of Christ crucified would be revealed. This doesn't mean that Paul accepted his thorn in the flesh as "the way things should be" or rejoiced in suffering for the sake of suffering. But his life of prayerful ministry was filled with the rich paradoxes of one who has been united to the crucified and risen Lord: "as sorrowful, yet always rejoicing; as poor, yet making many rich; as having nothing, and yet possessing everything" (2 Cor. 6:10).

Thus, as we petition in the context of praying for God's kingdom to come and God's will to be done, we do so in gratitude and joy and yet in grief and protest against the present evil age. We ask in gratitude to our Creator and King, who has given astonishingly good gifts—gifts of daily bread, gifts of a sublime creation that reflects in so many ways the beauty of the Creator; we ask in joy that God has become our Father through his covenant promise, and that in Christ, God has promised,

"'I will never leave you or forsake you.' So we can say with confidence, 'The Lord is my helper; I will not be afraid. What can anyone do to me?'" (Heb. 13:5–6). We ask for God's kingdom to come as ones who weep and lament and protest with Christ who wept for Jerusalem right before turning the tables in the temple in protest (Luke 19:41, 45–58). We ask for the kingdom to come with Christ who wept and lamented in Gethsemane, for in our praying we are called "to follow Jesus to Gethsemane, even when you don't understand why."[18] We pray as a Christ-shaped people for a Christ-shaped kingdom to come—one that does not bypass Gethsemane and the cross, even as it recognizes that Christ is none other than the Creator in whom "all things hold together" (Col. 1:17) and the Deliverer who has defeated death through his cross and resurrection. In praying for a Christ-shaped kingdom to come, we recognize that the cross was not a temporary stopping point on the way toward "victorious living," for we serve a King who is the Lamb of God, the crucified Lord whose power defies our sight. "Thy kingdom come." We should pray for healing. But as we lament and petition, we should not pray for the healing to defy the loving, cruciform path of our Savior but to conform us to it. In the words of N. T. Wright, "The Kingdom did indeed come with Jesus; it will fully come when the world is healed, when the whole creation finally joins in the song. But it must be Jesus's medicine; it must be Jesus's music. And the only way to be sure of that is to pray his prayer."[19]

8

In the Valley

*Toxins, Healing, and Strong Medicine
for Sinners*

What does it take to receive deep healing? Before my cancer diagnosis, when I went to the doctor I assumed that healing should usually come through a pill or maybe, if I were unlucky, an operation. But as I anticipated my stem cell transplant, I realized how superficial my view of healing was. I needed *strong medicine*. And ready or not, strong medicine meant poison. Strong poison. The main chemotherapy I was to receive as part of the transplant process was a derivative of mustard gas, a chemical weapon. There is no healing apart from walking through "the valley of the shadow of death" (Ps. 23:4 KJV).

> O LORD, heal me, for my bones are shaking with terror.
> My soul also is struck with terror,
>> while you, O LORD—how long?
>
> Turn, O LORD, save my life;
>> deliver me for the sake of your steadfast love. (Ps. 6:2–4)

131

I needed deliverance—rescue—from forces threatening my life. Healing was not going to come through a gentle pill. Ready or not, I was in the midst of a battle. I needed strong medicine. This chapter explores the strong medicine and deep healing of the stem cell transplant, and the way in which this intersects with the strong medicine and deep healing that we need as sinners in need of rescue.

Strong Medicine for Sinners

What does it take for sinners like us to receive deep healing? If we are to follow the direction of the New Testament, the psalms of lament give us unmistakable clues. After Psalm 22, with its poignant laments, "My God, My God, why have you forsaken me?," the most quoted Psalm in the New Testament is Psalm 69. This is a psalm of profound complaint and grief, a call for deliverance from enemies.

> I am weary with my crying;
>> my throat is parched.
> My eyes grow dim
>> with waiting for my God.
>
> More in number than the hairs of my head
>> are those who hate me without cause;
> many are those who would destroy me,
>> my enemies who accuse me falsely.
> What I did not steal
>> must I now restore? (Ps. 69:3–4)
>
>> At an acceptable time, O God,
>> in the abundance of your steadfast love, answer me.
> With your faithful help rescue me
>> from sinking in the mire;
> let me be delivered from my enemies
>> and from the deep waters. (Ps. 69:13–14)

Again and again, the psalm appeals to God's promise of "steadfast love" in a desperate cry for deliverance. It ends with a call to praise the

Lord, who will show himself faithful to his covenant promises to his chosen, adopted people. "For God will save Zion . . . the children of his servants shall inherit it, and those who love his name shall live in it" (69:35–36). In the New Testament, as strange as it may sound, this Psalm was repeatedly used to speak about the strong medicine that God uses to save sinners—the victory of Christ over enemies through his righteous suffering and the saving work of his faithful life and death vindicated in the resurrection.[1]

As the "strong medicine" of the transplant approached, I couldn't help but think of the strong medicine that sinners need for deep healing. In Mark 2:17, Jesus says, "Those who are well have no need of a physician, but those who are sick; I have come to call not the righteous but sinners." We are among the sick and sinful who need a doctor, a strong Savior. On January 10, 2013, I wrote the following in my CarePages.

I hope that you had a blessed Advent and Christmas celebration before entering into the new year. Our family's time was good, though with some times of real challenge—some tastes of joy, some of darkness. I've noticed how pastors often have to remind us that Christmas is a time of sadness for some—for instance, those who have lost a loved one or are facing particular challenges that make the pressure to constantly "be happy" at Christmas quite difficult. Pastors are right to give this reminder. This is actually not just a pastoral "add-on" to a Christmas holiday, but it points to an uncomfortable and little-noticed reality: recognition of the darkness of the fall and sin is inherent to the Christmas celebration itself. When the angel announces to the shepherds that "to you is born this day in the city of David a Savior, who is the Messiah, the Lord" (Luke 2:11), this is not only cause for celebration. It's an offense, both then and now. Who needs a Savior? Those who have tasted the darkness and need rescue. Christmas is a celebration not of our good will but of our Savior, because we need one. We're in the exile of the fall and sin, and we can't find our way home. We can't manufacture a solution on our own. Advent and Christmas should break through our illusions that we're okay on our own, that deep down we really don't need a Savior. We're in a mess, and we do need a Savior. That aspect of celebrating the coming of our Savior was particularly real to me this year.

Deep Sickness and Deep Healing in Christ

As the CarePages entry above indicates, the good news of the Great Physician, Jesus Christ, is also news of how deep our sickness is and how we need a very strong medicine for healing. Augustine reflects deeply on this strong medicine. We are corrupted with the sickness of pride. Thus, in Jesus Christ, God became incarnate, taking the form of a servant so that pride "might be healed. He came down and the Son of God became humble."[2] We need to see what health looks like—what a human covenant partner was intended to look like without the sickness of sin. "Because 'the Word was made flesh, and dwelt among us' (John 1:14), by the Nativity itself He made a salve by which the eyes of our heart may be wiped clean and we may be able to see His majesty through his lowliness. . . . His glory no one could see unless one were healed by the lowliness of his flesh." This is a costly medicine, indeed: incarnation, a life of obedience, cross, and resurrection. "He came in such a way that by his flesh he might extinguish the faults of the flesh and by his death he might kill death."[3]

Moreover, the medicine of the incarnation, life, death, and resurrection of Christ requires more than seeing a healthy "example" from a distance. In order for the medicine to be effective, we have to be nourished by Christ—to be *united* to him. For "Very truly, I tell you, unless you eat the flesh of the Son of Man and drink his blood, you have no life in you"; this feeding involves a life-giving abiding in union with Jesus Christ. "Those who eat my flesh and drink my blood abide in me, and I in them. Just as the living Father sent me, and I live because of the Father, so whoever eats me will live because of me" (John 6:53, 56–57). Wow. To take our medicine, we have to feed on Christ by the Spirit, as the one sent by the Father; we don't just pop a pill. We feed on Christ, abiding and dwelling in him, the Healer.

A Transplant and a Battle for Health

As my cancer doctors oriented me to the "strong medicine" of the transplant, I came to realize how the path to healing would require a battle, a brush with death followed by a rescue. As I wrote in my CarePages,

> The chemo regimen, and especially the stem cell transplant, is saturated with militaristic imagery. It's a chemo "battle," all part of a "fight with cancer." Military terms are used for various parts of the stem cell transplant process. And it fits. In a broad sense, the stem cell transplant is all about battle, extreme chemical warfare: when I enter the hospital in early March, I will receive an intensive chemo drug that is derived from the World War I chemical weapon mustard gas. In a sense, I'm not going into the hospital in order to have a stem cell transplant. I'm going into the hospital to receive heavy doses of toxins (read: poisons). These poisons would definitely kill me if there were not a way to revive me from it. My white blood counts will drop to around zero; I will have virtually no resistance to infection. You can't live like that. But with my own healthy stem cells transfused back into my body, they will eventually start to produce healthy white counts again. The stem cell transplant day is often called a "second birthday," since the intensive chemo brings one to the edge, and then stem cell transplant provides a way to live again.

> The rhetoric of a "war" on cancer is . . . interesting on several levels. Sometimes it has been used in a way that leads to patient overtreatment, with the killing of the cancer rather than the healing of the

patient being the main concern. But at other times, and I think in the case of my particular cancer, it is the latter—the use of heavy poisons is an act of mercy. Myeloma is an active, invasive cancer that requires hard-core treatment to push it into remission.

As the date for the transplant and hospital time approached, I was often asked about whether I was ready. I was scared, even though the mortality rate directly from a transplant is quite low. But I had never received a lethal dose of toxins before, and it seemed strange to call it "medicine."

I heard a friend refer to the intensive chemo treatment as "medicine." I literally broke out laughing. It is medicine in a certain sense, I explained, but it's actually poison. But of course, the boundary between medicine and poison is sometimes a thin one—particularly in cancer treatment.

While reading through John Calvin's reflections on the Psalms for devotional reading, I was struck by his ability to see that thin line between an apparently poisonous affliction and medicine in God's economy, God's way of working in the world. Calvin does this as he reflects on the line in Psalm 118 that "the Lord has chastened me severely, but he has not given me over to death." Calvin notes that when afflictions come to us, most of us think that God's paternal care is far from us. Yet "God always deals mercifully with his own people, so that his correction proves their cure." So although the psalmist speaks of the "chastisements" coming from God, "so far from being deadly, [they] serve the purpose of a medicine, which through it produce a temporary debility, rids us of our malady, and renders us healthy and vigorous."[4] (That sounds a bit like a stem cell transplant!) If we are really in need of a Savior, then we are in need of rescue, in need of strong medicine. In this

136

case, following the psalmist, Calvin thinks that afflictions that might appear poisonous on their own can actually bring life through the Father's hands.

. . . I didn't choose to enter into this battle, but I'm grateful to have a mighty and merciful God, made known in Christ, as a Savior and Deliverer in the midst of it.

The day before I entered the hospital to start the "warfare" that would wipe out my bone marrow, I sent to my CarePages supporters the following prayer, which I had adapted from another patient's prayer. Two days later, after having received the high-dose chemotherapy, my pastor would pray this as the "rescue plan" was administered—as the salmon-colored healthy stem cells were injected into my body. My partners in prayer on the CarePages were encouraged to pray this as well as part of a common, shared prayer.

This is the day that the Lord has made. Let us rejoice and be glad in it. (Ps. 118:24)

Most Merciful God, Father, Son, and Holy Spirit,

You spoke light and life into being with your word, saying, "'Let there be light'; and there was light" (Gen. 1:3). You created the "living creatures," and saw that it was good (1:20–21). You created humankind, and "saw everything that [you] had made, and indeed, it was very good" (Gen. 1:31).

You have done this through our Lord and Savior, Jesus Christ, for "all things came into being through him, and without him not one thing came into being" (John 1:3). Christ has come to a fallen world corrupted by sin, and we rejoice that "The light shines in the darkness, and the darkness did not overcome it" (John 1:5).

We come before you today, humbled by your great gift of life. You have given this to us as our almighty Creator, as our loving Father who sent Jesus Christ as light and life into the world. In your infinite wisdom, you planted tiny cells within our blood that can be used in your purposes to heal and renew. For giving scientists, physicians, and nurses the knowledge to use these cells for our well-being, we give you thanks.

Christ gave his life that we may have life, and by his wounds we are healed. We are grateful that we have been cleansed and renewed by the blood of Jesus Christ. We pray now that you would display your power in restoring health to Todd through the renewed blood that you are giving him through this transplant.

Today, we ask a special blessing on Todd as he receives these life-giving cells. Let him trust not in their power to heal apart from you but in and through your providential care. Grant Todd patience and hope as he waits for the restoration of body, mind, and spirit.

And now, send your Spirit upon Todd, and upon his renewed blood, bringing him and his family your love and healing power. We pray that you would use this transplant to push his cancer far away, into deep remission. We pray that you would grant Todd many more years with his family, with his vocation, in service to you and your kingdom. For the sake of your kingdom, and in the name of Jesus Christ, we pray, *Amen.*

Two days later, as I received the transplant, I felt remarkably good. I had the "strong medicine" of poison in my body, but it takes four to five days before its side effects become severe. I was tired, but I still read and wrote when I had strength. My nurses teased me about some of the scholarly tomes I was cracking open those days. I was also reflecting on what was happening theologically—the analogies (and lack thereof) between this strong medicine for the healing of my cancer and the even *stronger* medicine for healing in the gospel. On the day that I received the transplant, I composed and sent the following CarePages message from the hospital.

On "Second Birthday," New Life, and Analogies

So, today is my "second birthday," as they call it! [I tell about how my wife, Rachel, came with a "second birthday" cake after the transplant, and the nurses also brought cupcakes.] They call today the "second birthday" for patients because the cancer—and in particular, the high-dose chemo—would lead to death. But the transplant provides for a new beginning, a second chance at life.

As I approach this day, I've been thinking through what it is and what it isn't. To be honest, when I first heard the analogy of "second birthday" for the transplant, it made me a bit uncomfortable: from a theological perspective, I've already had a second birthday, a rebirth, and I continue to have an ongoing rebirth each day by the Spirit. I've also heard the intense chemo and transplant process described as "death and resurrection." I see some parallels, but the discontinuity is also striking. I may come close to death, but God willing, I won't experience it now. Even more important, the stem cell transplant won't initiate a resurrection—that is, a participation in Christ's own resurrection, one in which the body that is "raised is imperishable"—it is "raised in glory" (1 Cor. 15:42–43).

These analogies between the transplant process and the Spirit's work of rebirth, and of death and resurrection, do raise some concerns for me. First, I don't want my own experience with death and new life to be confused or paralleled too closely to the dying and rising of Christ. Our union with Christ in his death and resurrection is very real—it's a central feature of Christian identity. We have been united to Christ in his death and resurrection (e.g., Rom. 6:5). But our union with Christ's death and resurrection is shaped by what he has done, not by our own experience of "death" and "rebirth." Christ is the only one who has a life, death, and resurrection that is inherently redemptive. And that is good news. That *difference* between Christ and us, even in our union with him, is something to be cherished.

Recently I had a conversation with a hospital staff person who works a lot with cancer patients and who just underwent testing for a tumor that was discovered in her own body. It was benign. While happy with the results, she wondered, "Why me? I am so much older than many of my patients with active cancer. If I could take the cancer of a young patient to make them better, I would do so." In a similar way, after a quite emotional meeting at Western Theological Seminary in which I announced my cancer diagnosis to the faculty, a retired faculty member came up to me and said these words: "I wish it were me rather than you." The words were especially poignant, because I think he really meant it. He saw a young faculty colleague taking on a path that is much more expected for someone his own age. "No one has greater love than this, to lay down one's life for one's friends" (John 15:13).

What is key to recognize here, however, is that Jesus is not *just* teaching an ethic to lay down our life for our friends, as if we could save the world ourselves if we would just act in that way. His passage in John 15 is in the context of bearing fruit as we abide *in Christ*, the sole source for bearing fruit. My conversation partner expressed an admirable sentiment in wanting to take on the cancer of the young patients whom she knew. But her next words were telling: "But I can't take on their cancer." She can't be their redeemer. She can help others, even in a self-sacrificial way. But she can't "be Christ" to them. Christ alone is the redeemer. Christ is the source for our fruit-bearing, including our self-sacrificial fruit-bearing. Recognizing the *difference* between Christ and us is some of what it means to recognize and celebrate our union with Christ.

So, I had a second birthday today. But my real second birth was and is even better. In being "born from above" (John 3:7), the Spirit brings a life in Christ that not even bodily death can stop. I have the agents of life and death swimming around in my bloodstream right now in a pretty eerie way. But all of us live in the in-between time, when we have started to experience new life in Christ. But we also often act in the "old self," our dead self, according to Romans 6:6–10. Living into our true identities—as dead to the "old," sinful self, and alive in Christ—is a battle that each of us faces on a day-to-day level.

In the end, I sense that there are helpful ways to think through analogies between the "second birthday" and the rebirth that we have in Christ. But we have to be careful and remember that the analogy moves only one way: from Christ and Scripture to us. We are not redeemers. My encounter with the prospect of death and new life with the transplant is not redemptive in itself. Only the death and resurrection of Christ is redemptive, and by the Spirit we live in fellowship with Christ and bear the fruit of this wonderful union we have with him.

It's become popular to speak about Christians "becoming the hands and feet of Jesus" to people in need—a theme in Christian music, in churches, and so on.[5] But I'm afraid that, unintentionally, that way of speaking doesn't reckon with the strong medicine that sinners need. The hospital staff person got it right: we can't take on their cancer; we can't "be Jesus" to those around us. We can show love. We can mourn with those who mourn and rejoice with those who rejoice. But as we do all of this, we can do nothing higher than to be a witness to the King of the coming kingdom. Even on our "best days" we are not the very presence of Christ to the world—in ourselves, we are not the deep medicine that the world needs. We are ambassadors, witnesses giving a "sign" of the coming kingdom. We are united to Christ, the Great Healer, but we are not absorbed into him. While we are the body of Christ, we are subordinate to Christ as "the head of the church"—for he alone is "the Savior" that the world needs (Eph. 5:23).

Living between the Times, Living in Christ

We live in Christ, the strong medicine and the true healer, but this life in Christ is between two ages. Jesus Christ, the Great Physician, has already been victorious over sin, death, and the devil in his life, death, and resurrection. The kingdom has come in him. Yet we are still waiting for the promised kingdom to come in fullness. We *are* God's adopted children by the Spirit. But we are *still awaiting* our adoption and our final healing with tears and groaning. In the days following my "second birthday," I experienced those tears and groaning: frequent nausea, weakness, and dizziness, such that I could not even walk without help. With virtually no immune system, I was not able to receive visits from family members, who had colds during the Michigan winter. Yet as the book of Hebrews says, because of God's covenant promise "we have this hope, a sure and steadfast anchor of the soul" (Heb. 6:19). I needed an anchor during this time of waiting because it certainly did not feel like the new creation.

As I noted in the CarePages passage above, living between two ages means that "living into our true identities—as dead to the 'old,' sinful self, and alive in Christ—is a battle that each of us faces on a day-to-day level." John Calvin spoke about the implications of this in terms of a "double grace" that believers receive in union with Christ: "namely, that being reconciled to God through Christ's blamelessness, we may have in heaven instead of a Judge a gracious Father; and secondly, that sanctified by Christ's spirit we may cultivate blamelessness and purity of life."[6] In the first of the two inseparable but distinct gifts of the double grace, we are acquitted of our sin through Christ's righteousness (justification); thus, when sinners are justified by faith, this is based not on "the righteousness of works" but on the fully sufficient righteousness of Christ.[7] In this way, we are legally and presently adopted in Christ; we are welcomed into the household of God, able to call God our Father by the Spirit. In the second gift, we receive new life, so that through the Spirit's empowerment we can grow into our new, adopted identity in Christ. In contrast to justification, the Spirit's

142

gift of sanctification, which God accomplishes in us to "restore in us the image of God," does "not take place in one moment or one day or one year." For although we *are* already in Christ, in this living in the "in-between time" we have a long journey of growth in Christ and a battle of daily repentance, empowered by the Spirit: "Through continual and sometimes even slow advances God wipes out in his elect the corruptions of the flesh, cleanses them of guilt, consecrates them to himself as temples renewing all their minds to true purity that they may practice repentance throughout their lives and know that this warfare will end only at death."[8]

In this way, the Christian life is one in which we live in the midst of Paul's contrasting tenses: those united to Christ "have died" and yet are entreated to "put to death, therefore" sinful desires (Col. 3:3, 5); "we know that our old self was crucified" and "we have died with Christ," yet we are admonished to "put on the Lord Jesus Christ, and make no provision for the flesh" (Rom. 6:6, 8; 13:14). Paul uses the indicative (that Christians have been united to Christ in his death and resurrection) as the basis for the imperative (to "put on Christ").[9] Thus we are not to look to ourselves in order to find the resources to be holy. The source for our new life—a life of putting to death (repentance) and coming to life in the ways of God—is Jesus Christ and our new identity in union with him, received through the Spirit. To utilize a favorite biblical image from Luther, as the church we are indeed the bride of Christ (Eph. 5:25–27), yet we still wait for that identity to be fully consummated at the "marriage supper of the Lamb" (Rev. 19:9). Luther insists that the eyes of faith look to the promise of God in Jesus Christ and our union with him. "Though she is weighed down by many evils, nevertheless she has a Bridegroom who takes all her evils upon himself and communicates his power and glory to her."[10] When sin and the devil plague her, the bride of Christ looks to Christ, her Bridegroom and says, "I have the righteousness of the Bridegroom. It is mine, so be quiet." And "when sorrow plagues her, she says: 'In my Bridegroom is life, grace, peace, joy, salvation. These things are mine, because Christ is mine. Then why do you frighten me?'"

Thus, our hope of living in this "in-between time" is not in ourselves but in Jesus Christ and the forgiveness and new life that we receive in him. We look to God's promises, seeking to live into the new identity given to us by the Spirit in Christ. We are sinners. But in being united to Christ by the Spirit, we are—and will be—Christ's bride who "possesses with fullest right life, righteousness, grace, and salvation in Christ."[11]

Engraftment in Transplants, and Engraftment into Christ

Our hope in this "in-between time" is not just an idea from an ancient book or a story about a person who died long ago. This hope is a present reality because by the Spirit we are actually united to the living Christ, engrafted into him by the Spirit. After a few weeks of struggling with the side effects of the high-dose chemotherapy, I was released from the hospital to spend a week in a sterile cancer lodge. This lodge provided me a place to stay while I was still immunocompromised but did not need twenty-four-hour nursing care. From the lodge, I could put on a mask and walk to the hospital each day for ongoing care. After some tests, my doctors were delighted because of the "engraftment" that took place in my bones. With thanksgiving to God, I shared with my CarePages prayer partners the good news about my engraftment.

In a chapel service at Western Seminary before the transplant process,
I spoke these words of complaint and petition from Psalm 102:2–3.

Do not hide your face from me
    in the day of my distress.
Incline your ear to me;
    answer me speedily in the day when I call.
For my days pass away like smoke,
    and my bones burn like a furnace.

144

I think that it is fair to say that the Lord has heard the cry of complaint and petition for this part of my cancer journey. My bones were "burned" two weeks ago with high-dose chemotherapy, but they have begun a remarkably strong recovery. My bone marrow has started to produce white blood cells with vigor.

Writing from the cancer lodge, I went on to speak about two different life-giving engraftments that I received.

What is engraftment? The term itself derives from the world of horticulture—grafting a branch onto a plant in such a way that the branch is incorporated into the plant, becoming a part of the plant itself. As a metaphor, "engraftment" is a way to speak about a powerful incorporation and union: that which was separate is made one, permanently incorporated into that with which it is united.

Before the stem cell transplant, I had to sign a consent form that gave an overview of the risks of the transplant. At one point, the form stated that if "engraftment" did not occur, it could be fatal. Why is that the case? The healthy stem cells were transfused into my blood in the transplant process, but at first they just floated around in my blood. If they had not engrafted—not united and become incorporated—into my bone marrow, then the "rescue plan" from the high-dose chemo would have failed. Thus, I would have taken a mustard gas–derived chemo drug with no antidote. It's not surprising that the failure of engraftment could—probably would—lead to death. Because of the death-dealing powers of the chemo, the consent form probably could have used a simple formula: no engraftment means no life.

My medical team has been rejoicing that my engraftment has happened quickly, and also with vigor. They have repeatedly

145

congratulated me about how well things are going, since the engraftment started several days ago. But of course, while I share in their rejoicing, I deserve no credit whatsoever for this: engraftment is something that happened *to* me. It was not from any foresight or hard effort of my own.

When I was writing my dissertation at Harvard, I came to love the word and the concept of "engraftment." Why? I was writing on the biblical teaching of union with Christ and how John Calvin in particular received and developed that teaching. The concept itself is rich: in Romans 11:13–24, Paul uses the horticultural imagery from the Old Testament to speak about how gentile believers have been graciously engrafted into the people of God. In the Gospel of John, Christ himself speaks about how he is the vine and his disciples are the branches attached to him who can bear fruit only by abiding in him (15:1–8). For "apart from me you can do nothing" (15:5). No engraftment means no life.

It was also a favorite image for John Calvin in speaking about how we are united to Christ. In addition to the John 15 passage, Calvin used the image of engrafting in his translation and comments on Romans 6:5. Instead of what the NIV translates as "united" below, Calvin translates as "engrafted": "If we have been united with him in a death like his, we will certainly also be united with him in a resurrection like his." About this act of being "united/engrafted" to Christ in Romans 6:5, Calvin writes, "Grafting designates not only a conformity of example, but a secret union, by which we are joined to him; so that he, reviving us by his Spirit, transfers his own virtue [i.e., "power"] to us. Hence as the graft has the same life or death in common with the tree into which it is engrafted, so it is reasonable that we should be partakers of the life no less than of the death of Christ; for if we are engrafted according to the likeness of Christ's death, which was not without a resurrection, then our death shall not be without a resurrection."[12] In other words, we don't just follow Jesus's example as disciples from a distance. We have been united and

146

joined to him, engrafted into Christ so that our life comes from Christ, received by the Spirit. Thus, we are not only united with Christ in his death (and thus we have died to our "old self," Rom. 6:8–11); we are also united with Christ in his resurrection, anticipated by the new life we receive by the Spirit.

As Christians, we often fall into the trap of thinking that the Christian life is up to us "trying hard" on our own to follow Christ's example. But that vision undermines the incredible gift of engraftment into Christ. As Calvin says about this gift, "Christ, having been made ours, makes us sharers with him in the gifts with which he has been endowed. We do not, therefore, contemplate him outside ourselves from afar in order that his righteousness may be imputed to us but because we put on Christ and are engrafted into his body—in short because he deigns to make us one with him."[13]

We are engrafted into Christ and, simultaneously, into his body, the church. In Christ we find our only hope and comfort; in Christ we receive both forgiveness and new life. And it's not because we tried really hard and pulled off "engraftment." It's because by the Spirit, we have been united to Christ through faith. Rather than following Christ from a distance, we can display the fruit of the Spirit in our lives as ones who have actually been engrafted into Christ. While no engraftment means no life, engraftment into Christ means abundant life.

Today I am thankful for both engraftments—the one that began a few days ago, and even more so for the profound engraftment into Christ and his body that has been, and continues to be, a great gift. I didn't do anything to deserve either one; I can just give thanks.

All of us need strong medicine. We don't just need a vitamin; we don't just need a bandage to cover a flesh wound. We need *strong* medicine— we need death and new life in order to be healed, to have God's created goodness restored, and to find reconciliation in our loving communion with God and neighbor. We find our medicine in union—union with Jesus Christ, God incarnate, who lived a truly human life of humble obedience that led to death and then resurrected life. When we face suffering and then lament to God—even blaming and accusing God—asking for the deliverance that he alone can provide, we start to look to the Great Physician for the strong medicine that we need. Thus, even when we feel abandoned in "spiritual trials, sorrow, grief, and anguish of heart," God can use these as "the medicines with which God purges away sin" (Luther).[14] This purging actually restores true human health; it is a coming to life in Christ through the "medicine" of forgiveness and new life (Calvin).[15] For if we stay in ourselves, we stay in our sickness: no engraftment, no life. But in looking to Christ "who is your life" (Col. 3:4), we find our health; in abiding in Christ, in feeding on Christ, we receive a medicine deep and strong enough that we will never go into relapse. For as ones who have been united to Christ, the Great Physician and the strong medicine himself, we receive "a new birth into a living hope," an "inheritance" as God's adopted children "that is imperishable, undefiled, and unfading" (1 Pet. 1:3–4).

9

The Light of Perfect Love in the Darkness

God's Impassible Love in Christ

Sometimes suffering feels like a free fall rather than a swing down to the valley on a rope that will bring me back up to safety. My doctors were delighted at my body's response to the transplant, and I was giving thanks to God. I was thankful to be alive. I knew that many others (with cancer or other trials) have had much rockier roads than my own, and that in a matter of months I would be returning to "the land of the living." But to my own surprise, much of my deepest grieving came after this good news. I recall lying on my bed in the cancer lodge, crying aloud, when the thought came to mind: my life would never be the same—I would receive low-dose chemo for as long as my remissions last and frequent cancer tests "until" it returns. When it returns, I will need more intensive treatment—perhaps more high-dose chemo and a stem cell transplant, donor transplant, or other aggressive treatments to counter the cancer. As I thought about returning to my "normal life," I felt more alienated than ever. How was I to respond to ordinary questions like "How are you?" and "How have you been?" How was I to look toward the future—for my family, for my vocation? "My eye grows dim through sorrow. Every day I call on you, O LORD; I spread out my hands to you" (Ps. 88:9). I feared for my children, that they would lose their father midcourse in their childhood. The good news about my transplant didn't take this fear away.

In the midst of this experience were three other dynamics: very deep, heavy fatigue; isolation; and two friends dying of cancer. For months after the transplant, my fatigue was so powerful that my body was deeply exhausted for most of the day. Everyday tasks—particularly interpersonal interactions—were painful: they seemed to require energy that I didn't have, frequently leaving me with sharp headaches. The second factor was isolation: for the first two months, I was quarantined from public places because of my compromised immune system, isolated from all but family members and an occasional visitor who swore they did not have a bit of sickness and who underwent a regimen of handwashing. When a visitor did come, it took only about twenty minutes before I was too exhausted to think or speak coherently. In that time, of course, I could not even scratch the surface about "how I was doing." Although I deeply appreciated the companionship of my family, I still felt isolated. Third, during this time of recovery, I had two friends with cancer reach the end of the line for their treatment, moving from experimental chemotherapy to palliative care, to dying, to death. It all happened so quickly. I was in remission, but for what? To wait around for this to happen to me, just as it happened to my friends? At certain moments, while other people's lives seemed to be moving ahead at full speed, mine seemed to be spinning in the direction of my dying and dead friends. Rather than reentering my previous, purposeful life, was I just to lament with the psalmist that I am "set apart with the dead, like the slain who lie in the grave" (Ps. 88:5 NIV)?

To top it off, when I received notes or phone calls, they quite universally rejoiced at the news of my good progress. I genuinely rejoiced with them, but I was also grieving deeply. My news was good—why was I grieving? It didn't seem fitting that I would be grieving at this point in the process, just when it looked like I was through the valley of death and returning to "regular life." It would be a "new normal," as the doctors say. But there was nothing "normal" about it. It felt like a new place of isolation, a new place of being misunderstood, a new place of living in fear.

During my time in quarantine, I sent out the following CarePages entry after updating my prayer partners on an emergency room visit due to some symptoms I was experiencing.

Living as a Mortal Creature before God

We don't know when we will die. We have no power over that. As Ecclesiastes says, "As no one has power over the wind to contain it, so no one has power over the time of their death" (8:8 NIV).

This reality is felt in a particular way by cancer patients who have incurable cancers, like my own. While I rejoice in all of my unexpected progress, none of my progress does anything to "undo" the larger picture, namely, that my cancer is expected to return after remission. We hope and pray for a long remission. But in the meantime, I'll be taking tests frequently to see whether it has returned. And the disease is more difficult to treat after it returns. All of us will die, and "no one has power over the time of their death." But I suspect that the practice of taking a test every three to six months to see whether this death-dealing disease has returned will change the way that I live.

Last Friday in the emergency room, I became immersed in an excellent book recommended by my colleague, Carol Bechtel: *Getting Involved with God: Rediscovering the Old Testament* by Ellen Davis. In particular, I found her treatment of the books of Ecclesiastes and Job helpful and illuminating.

As Davis points out in her chapter on Ecclesiastes, "The reality of death conditions every moment of life."[1] Again and again,

Ecclesiastes returns to the point: "All go to one place; all are from the dust, and all turn to dust again" (3:20). There is a profound realism—and pessimism—to the book of Ecclesiastes. But along with this is the theme that *because* we are small, mortal creatures, we need to name as "vanity" our ambitions for fame and fortune (1:8–11) and enter into our daily, creaturely activities as gifts from the singular Giver of life: "There is nothing better for mortals than to eat and drink, and find enjoyment in their toil. This also, I saw, is from the hand of God; for apart from him who can eat or who can have enjoyment?" (2:24–25).

As Davis points out, the book of Job shows a path of how one can enter into the daily activities of life after facing the realities of death and suffering. Having lost his children to death early in the book, Job takes on the task of raising more children. These children do not replace the ones he lost (as if they could be replaced!). Instead, according to Davis, the "clearest expression of the renewal of Job's mind" is "his willingness to have more children." For "how can he [Job] open himself again to the terrible vulnerability of loving those whom he cannot protect against suffering and untimely death?"[2] Job knows the reality of loss, of suffering, of mortality. And yet he pours himself into the lives of fragile, mortal children.

In many ways, I don't identify with the story of Job; in addition to sickness, he lost his sons, daughters, livestock, and livelihood. I feel so tremendously blessed with a loving family, a vocation at a seminary that I love, and so many supports. But there is something about facing one's mortality—and knowing that it will be faced frequently in the future—that changes how you live: there is both a tremendous joy and a tremendous risk in investing in the lives of other mortals. When I read stories to Neti or throw balls with Nathaniel, I sometimes wonder, *What will the future hold? Will I be around when they are in middle school, in high school?* Even in returning to the "land of the living" after my quarantine, a part of me thinks about my own mortality and the mortality of those I serve. Is it worth pouring my

152

energy into other mortals as a mortal myself? All of us will die. And I, as a mortal, cannot be anyone's savior. I'm not at the center of the universe, after all. God is.

Yet I pray that, as Job does in his restoration, I can give myself to loving my children and the other mortals around me. And, of course, Job is just a shadow in comparison to Christ himself, whose sacrificial life and death shows us not only how to "move on" after considering our mortality but what love itself is: "This is how we know what love is: Jesus Christ laid down his life for us. And we ought to lay down our lives for our brothers and sisters" (1 John 3:16 NIV). Living as a mortal means realizing that the future is not under our control and that each day—with its relationships and its tasks—comes as a gift. It means living as a creature who will die. But as ones who belong to Christ, we can have confidence that living as mortal creatures need not lead us to a paralyzing fear of death; rather, Christ, who shows the way to life, gave his life away in love and shows us what love is. We belong to Christ, not to ourselves. Thus, let us confidently "lay down our lives" in love.

During this time, I came to realize that although my grief was often sharp, my laments were still prayers of hope rather than complete despair. Even reading the book of Ecclesiastes felt freeing, refreshing—in recognizing the "vanity" of much in creaturely life, I realized that I was not in a free fall but in the hands of the Creator. Praying with the psalmist, I knew that I was not a pioneer plunging into the darkness, even though at times nothing seemed to be able to undo the immense loss. "My God, my God, why have you forsaken me? Why are you so far from helping me, from the words of my groaning?" (Ps. 22:1). Although the psalmist feels "forsaken," that lament itself suggests that the poet *belongs* to God, his helper; otherwise there would be no cry of complaint.[3] It is, ultimately, a cry of hope in the darkness that pivots on God's promise. Indeed, as strange as it may seem, I think that John

Calvin is right when he claims that even the most bitter laments of the Psalms are, in fact, "among the unutterable groanings of which Paul makes mention in Romans 8:26."[4] For "the Spirit himself intercedes for us with groanings too deep for words" (ESV).

We Are Not Pioneers in the Darkness

Even in the darkness of pain and alienation, the God of the covenant truly knows his people and has them in his hands. "Even before a word is on my tongue, O LORD, you know it completely. You hem me in, behind and before, and lay your hand upon me" (Ps. 139:4–5). We are not in a free fall; we are not pioneers in the darkness. The God of the Psalms is not a distant God. Likewise, this same God offers priestly mediation in Christ that is not distant from us in our darkest moments. "For we do not have a high priest who is unable to sympathize with our weaknesses, but we have one who in every respect has been tested as we are, yet without sin" (Heb. 4:15). For "in the days of his flesh, Jesus offered up prayers and supplications, with loud cries and tears, to the one who was able to save him from death, and he was heard because of his reverent submission" (Heb. 5:7). Our own "loud cries and tears" are not those of ones blazing new trails into grief; they are a Spirit-enabled sharing in the suffering of the One who has plunged even deeper into the darkness than us—yet not without hope.

Thus, when on the cross Jesus cries with the psalmist, "My God, my God, why have your forsaken me?," this is a cry of desolation that shows us that when we pray this ourselves, we are not pioneers; we are not in a free fall. It is a cry of unspeakable anguish and yet profound hope because in Christ the covenant God himself has taken on our human suffering, even our sufferings of alienation and dread. In this moment on the cross, Jesus Christ—as the embodiment of the true Israel and the new Adam—takes on the exile and forsakenness of humanity in order to exhaust it;[5] desolation itself is emptied of its finality by the Son's assumption of human misery in a faithful, covenantal lament.[6] The Heidelberg Catechism interprets Christ's "descent to hell" in the

154

Apostles' Creed as the redemptive act accomplished through Christ's deep lament.

Q. Why does the creed add, "He descended to hell"?

A. To assure me during attacks of deepest dread and temptation that Christ my Lord, by suffering unspeakable anguish, pain, and terror of soul, on the cross but also earlier, has delivered me from hellish anguish and torment.[7]

We need not fear that our "deepest dread" puts us onto a path that has not been walked before. It has been walked by the Man of Sorrows, the Lamb of God, the great High Priest who identifies with our terrors in order to heal them. In the words of fourth-century church father Ambrose, "Even as His death made an end of death, and His stripes healed our scars, so also His sorrow took away our sorrow." Jesus Christ, God incarnate, cries the prayer of abandonment of the psalmist in Psalm 22, who "speaks, bearing with Him my terrors, for when we are in the midst of dangers we think ourselves abandoned by God."[8] Jesus Christ shows the ultimate fulfillment of God's unrelenting, *hesed* love and faithfulness that the psalmists repeatedly testify to. "O give thanks to the LORD, for he is good, for his steadfast love endures forever" (Ps. 136:1). As a perfect expression of God's enduring love, Jesus Christ died, was raised, and "intercedes for us," such that "neither death, nor life, nor angels, nor rulers, nor things present, nor things to come, nor powers, nor height, nor depth, nor anything else in all creation, will be able to separate us from the love of God in Christ Jesus our Lord" (Rom. 8:34, 38–39). In a deeply paradoxical way, full of a mystery that blinds by its brightness, Jesus Christ, the God-human, displays the love of God—Father, Son, and Holy Spirit—by taking on our human suffering and terror. Christ, the God-human, takes on the path of human suffering so that we are not pioneers in the darkness, so that we are not in a free fall. Instead, even when our suffering seems senseless, even when we feel like we are in a free fall, we can look to Christ to see, hear, and taste that we are still in the ever-faithful, ever-loving hands of God.

155

In a sense I am expressing quite common Christian doctrine that has been taught through the centuries, as we will see below. However, among both academic theologians and in aspects of popular Christian piety today, there is often a quite different message: in his cry on the cross, the Son was abandoned by the Father; Christ did not give a lament that is undergirded by trust and ends in healing our "deepest dread." Some would say that God is taken off guard by our calamities, so God is hurt just like we are—thus we are left without assurance that we are *not* pioneers in the darkness. Some say that God's love means that "suffering" is an eternal attribute of the divine—as if *God* were in a free fall, rather than God lovingly responding to our fall and misery by taking on our human suffering in Christ and delivering us from its debilitating effects. Some say that rather than freely entering into our human condition of suffering in order to redeem and deliver us, God actually *needs* a suffering world in order to be divine. All of these theological issues come into focus in Christ's cry of lament on the cross, the climax of all biblical laments. And the concrete, experiential consequences of all of this for sufferers is profound.

I believe that in discerning the significance of Christ's lament on the cross, we need to consider a doctrine called divine impassibility. The doctrine finds its grounding in biblical and theological reasoning that takes seriously the larger biblical, covenantal context for Christ's cry of lament. And, rightly articulated, it provides profound comfort and encouragement for those who feel like they are in a free fall, as I have felt during my attempt to reenter the land of the living. Personally, I don't have the luxury of feeling sorry for God or settling for a God that is less than the biblical God of deliverance. In Christ, God has taken on our human suffering and grief and desolation, pioneering his way through it, overcoming its ultimate sting. And all of this flows from the voluntary, unrelenting, covenant love of Father, Son, and Holy Spirit. This provides the context for a biblical, although paradoxical, view of Christ's cry on the cross as an aspect of the saving work of his life, death, and resurrection.

Divine Impassibility: The Personal yet Unrelenting Love of God

How should we respond to the sense that we may be charting new paths of terror where God's love cannot reach us? The doctrine of impassibility points to the backbone of God's steady love that both takes on our human terror and overcomes it in Christ. But in order to see how this is the case, we do need to work with some definitions. What is divine impassibility?

The doctrine of divine impassibility is the belief that God has no "passions"—that is, disordered affections that could make his loving being and action ebb and flow. God's affections and actions are utterly consistent with his identity as the covenant Lord, thus the Lord who freely enters into covenantal relations with creatures is never blindsided by creatures or manipulated by them. Instead, God loves in fullness and has the appropriate relational, affective responses to creation: to delight in the goodness of creation and in obedience; to have compassion on the suffering and hear their cry; to grieve over the creation's self-destructive sin; and to be angry in response to evil, injustice, and wickedness. In this way, the doctrine of impassibility holds together two truths at once: while it is true and right to say that God loves, delights, grieves, and is jealous, there is also a fundamental difference and distinction between God's affections and our own creaturely ones.[9] God is *perfectly* vibrant in his affections"—unlike our own emotional lives, God's affections are never distorted through sinful, disordered passions.[10]

Thus, while we are to cherish and utilize these God-given ways of portraying how God relates to the world, we should also avoid thinking that "love," "grief," "wrath," or "jealousy" mean exactly the same thing for God as they do for us (what theologians call a "univocal" treatment of these terms).[11] Unlike the love, grief, wrath, and jealousy that we see and experience with other humans, God's affections are perfect, self-derived expressions of his faithful covenant love. When tragedy hits, we are likely to be reeling in surprise. You might say, "I was not myself." In contrast, God's affections are *always* in accord with his holy and gracious character. While our own emotional responses are often manipulated by others or caused by circumstances that make us act "not like ourselves," God is never less than the true, covenant Lord in any moment. Thus, there is a fundamental difference between God's affections and our own because God is God and we are not. For example, while God condemns human jealousy (1 Cor. 3:3), God is righteously jealous when his people engage in idolatry (Exod. 20:5). There is an analogy but also a distinction between the two notions of "jealousy."[12] For God is not growing or self-actualizing; in his delight, grief, wrath, and jealousy, God acts in perfect, untainted love. The perfection of God's character and action makes his promise trustworthy, making him a refuge for those who call to him in need. "This God—his way is perfect; the promise of the LORD proves true; he is a shield for all who take refuge in him" (Ps. 18:30).

The classical Christian teaching of divine impassibility is often caricatured as a doctrine that makes God apathetic and unresponsive; rightly construed, however, the opposite is the case. In the words of Thomas McCall,

> Perfect love, rather than being incompatible with impassibility, *demands* impassibility. Love that is passible fluctuates. Love that is passible gets caught up in the "heat of the moment." Love that is passible is subject to greater and lesser degrees of intensity. Love that is passible could, then, strengthen or weaken. To affirm impassibility, then, precisely denies that any of these things are true of God. Impassibility means that God's love is *absolutely* steadfast and perfect.[13]

On the one hand, this teaching is a negative one: God's love is *not* like human love in its mood swings, growth and diminishment, peaks and valleys. But it is a positive one as well: God's *hesed* love, the constant focus of the psalmist and brought to fulfillment in Christ, is the expression of the Triune God's unified, perfect love for creation. In its best articulations, it was not a doctrine that was just imported wholesale from Greek philosophy but refined in the furnace of debates about biblical exegesis in the course of developing ecumenical confessions

158

about the Trinity and Christ in the fourth and fifth centuries.[14] In other words, it is a biblical and ecumenical doctrine: while it reflects the Old Testament testimony to God's faithful, covenant love, a Christian doctrine of impassibility is forged in light of the New Testament witness to the deep paradoxes of the great and transcendent God who takes on humanity in the birth, life, death, and resurrection of Christ—at once truly God and truly human.

Divine impassibility maintains that Scripture speaks to us truly, even if analogically, in attributing emotions to God. Some think that the doctrine implies that God lacks "love, mercy, anger, hate, or (indeed!) pleasure," but historically, the doctrine insists that God "has all these relations to the world order. The exclusion of 'passions' from the divine being never implied the absence of 'affections.'"[15] Indeed, right after the Westminster Confession of Faith affirms impassibility, it speaks of the steadfast appropriateness of God's "loving, gracious, merciful, long-suffering" acts in relation to obedience, sin, and injustice.[16] How can these fit together? Consider the common scriptural example of God's wrath toward sinful rebellion. Is this wrath a loss of God's temper, a fuming vengeance, or a competing divine attribute that is in tension with God's love? Divine impassibilists would say no—even God's wrath is an expression of God's ordered, holy love. As Eastern Orthodox theologian Paul Gavrilyuk states, "It is precisely because God is impassible, i.e., free of uncontrollable vengeance, that repentant sinners may approach him without despair. Far from being a barrier to divine care and loving-kindness, divine impassibility is their very foundation."[17] In the words of Roman Catholic theologian Thomas Weinandy, impassibility is a denial that God's love is subject to change like human love, precisely because his love is already perfect; God's love is already fully actualized in his action, and the impassible God can be properly called "passionate" because "his will is fully and wholly fixed on the good as loved." "God cannot become more passionate or loving by actualizing, as human beings do, some further potential and so become more passionate or loving. . . . God is impassible precisely because he is supremely passionate and cannot become any more passionate."[18]

159

"God Is Suffering with You": Reassuring to a Human Sufferer?

The topic of divine impassibility came up a surprising number of times in notes that I received and in conversations about my illness. I recall receiving a greeting card with printed text from a well-known Christian author that sought to provide reassurance. "Does God hurt when you do? Absolutely." I sense that the person sending the card was seeking to say, "God *knows* you with intimacy in your suffering and has *compassion* on you in suffering." With the psalmists, I heartily concur. But this message and other messages claiming that "God is suffering with you" don't quite say that. They move closer to presenting a God who just reflects and mirrors what I'm feeling—like a Rogerian therapist. It sounds as if God were reeling in hurt and surprise from cancer just like I was: apparently, all that the suffering need is a God of identification and solidarity.

Yet even this identification (of God "hurting" with me) is not a true identification. As I've come to realize anew during my cancer treatment, pain and suffering is not an idea, an abstraction. It is not less than a *bodily* reality. This is obvious for some of the pain that I've experienced—the sharp pain of mouth sores, the exhaustion of deep fatigue, the sting of another injection—but it's also true of my emotional pain. When I was in anguish for the sake of my young children, this was not just a "thought" hovering above me but an experience of my whole body—tightened muscles, shallow breath, tears from my eyes. Indeed, as Elaine Scarry has argued, pain is a wound inseparable from the concrete bodily experience itself. "Physical pain has no voice."[19] Of course, we seek to express our pain—with cries, with metaphors, with stories—but Scarry's book shows how those linguistic expressions always fall short. Human suffering is inseparable from bodily pain, not just an "idea" that can float free of a body. But is a human body a part of God's divine nature? If we say no (as I and most Christians would), then the flat assertion that "God suffers" becomes a mere abstraction, a dark enigma, rather than an illuminating mystery. The notion of God as Spirit "suffering" in a nonbodily or nonhuman way provides me no solace, companionship, or identification. I believe that God knows me in my suffering in a perfect, loving intimacy. But to say instead that "God suffers with me" leaves me *isolated* in my bodily suffering rather than bringing God close to me in suffering and pointing toward suffering's healing.

However, for the vast majority of church history, most theologians have insisted that in the incarnation, God takes on precisely a bodily, human suffering in Christ. The Son assumes *human suffering and death* in the incarnation in order to conquer suffering and death and empty them of their ultimacy. When do the biblical writers ever provide assurance, like my greeting card did, by saying, "God is hurting with you"? That is an act of speech that has become common in our day but is not employed by the biblical writers. It is true that God embraces us in our suffering with perfect compassion. Indeed, in Christ we see a fulfillment of the Suffering Servant portrayed in Isaiah: "a man of sorrows, and acquainted with grief" (53:3 KJV). In Christ, the High Priest who is able "to sympathize with our weaknesses" (Heb. 4:15), God identifies with human sorrow, grief, and suffering. But our hope is not that God is overtaken by suffering in the same way that we are. We hope because in Christ, God has taken on human suffering and death so that they are emptied of their ultimate sting.

The Paradoxical Love of God in Christ

When the notion of God's suffering is moved from a vague abstraction to the mystery of the incarnation—that in Christ, the impassible God becomes one with suffering flesh in order to heal it—we are moved toward paradoxical words of worship, such as in Charles Wesley's hymn.

> And can it be that I should gain
> An interest in the Savior's blood?
> Died He for me, who caused His pain—
> For me, who Him to death pursued?

Amazing love! How can it be,
That Thou, my God, shouldst die for me?
Amazing love! How can it be,
That Thou, my God, shouldst die for me?

'Tis mystery all: th'Immortal dies:
Who can explore His strange design?
In vain the firstborn seraph tries
To sound the depths of love divine.

Because of the unity of the person of Jesus Christ, our Savior, we can worshipfully speak of "the immortal" that "dies"—the transcendent God taking on death for our sake.[20] But note that it is "the immortal" God. Wesley's paradox hinges on the union of a holy, transcendent God with the suffering, dying humanity of the person of Jesus Christ. Suffering and dying are not internal to the life of God—that would muddle the biblical paradox of Jesus Christ, "the one mediator between God and humankind," who "gave himself a ransom for all" (1 Tim. 2:5–6). For "the Word was God," and this same Word, through whom "all things came into being," "became flesh and lived among us" (John 1:1, 3, 14). The Creator himself takes on human flesh, uniting himself to it, dwelling among us as the perfect embodiment of God's covenant law and promises and becoming "obedient to the point of death—even death on a cross" (Phil. 2:8). In this way, the Triune God "reconciled us to himself through Christ" (2 Cor. 5:18). For God "made him to be sin who knew no sin, so that in him we might become the righteousness of God" (2 Cor. 5:21).

Thus it is essential that God is still God in the assumption of the suffering flesh and soul of Christ. In the words of the fourth-century bishop Gregory of Nazianzus, in the incarnation God the Son "remained what he was; what he was not, he assumed."[21] Because it is the transcendent God who assumes humanity in the incarnation, "the unassumed is the unhealed, but what is united with God is also being saved." Thus our bodily, human suffering is redeemed because God has assumed a bodily, human suffering in the incarnation. "He is weakened, wounded—yet he cures every disease and every weakness." "He has

162

united with himself all that lay under condemnation, in order to release it from condemnation."[22]

In the fifth century, the ecumenical Council of Chalcedon gave testimony to the paradoxical mystery of Christ by holding unflinchingly to the integrity of Christ's divine and human natures while firmly affirming the oneness of Christ's person. Christ's natures "undergo no confusion, no change, no division, no separation; at no point was the difference between the natures taken away through the union." In accord with this integrity of the natures, the council condemns priests who "dare to say that the divinity of the Only-begotten is passible."[23] Thus, for a Chalcedonian Christology, "God, as God, does not replicate what we, as humans, suffer. Yet in the incarnation God, remaining God, participates in our condition to the point of the painful death on the cross. Remaining impassible, God chooses to make the experiences of his human nature fully his own."[24] Chalcedon does not seek to rationalistically "solve" the many puzzles surrounding the person and work of Christ; instead, it points the church to the sharply paradoxical New Testament witness to the incarnation and cross of Christ while affirming the Easter hope that suffering and death have not only been assumed in Christ but also conquered through him.

God against God, or a God of Steadfast Love?

But some move quite stridently away from this paradoxical, two-nature approach to Christ confessed at Chalcedon. One very influential modern theologian, Jürgen Moltmann, insists that when Jesus laments with Psalm 22 on the cross, this is an event of "abandonment" between "God and God." "The abandonment on the cross which separates the Son from the Father is something which takes place within God."[25] Ironically, by asserting that Christ's cry of abandonment is rejected by the Father, Moltmann displaces the way in which Jesus's cry from Psalm 22 is one of solidarity with other human sufferers. He loses a key insight that can be retained only by emphasizing the fully human cry of Jesus on the cross. "Jesus, in lifting up the lament from Psalm 22,

163

is situating himself directly within that long line of servants who have suffered unjustly for God's sake and whom God will *not* abandon."[26] In contrast, Moltmann asserts, "What happened on the cross was an event between God and God. It was a deep division in God himself."[27]

To make this consistent, Moltmann realizes that this means that God needs the world in order to be God (what theologians call "panentheism"). And ultimately, since God is love, and love always involves suffering for Moltmann, God also needs suffering in order to be God.[28] For Moltmann, the impassible God does not take on the suffering body and soul of Christ in order to heal suffering from his plenitude of free, divine love; rather, in a way that flattens the biblical paradox of the incarnation, God must have the world in order to be God—and if God is to be a loving God, he must suffer whenever humanity suffers. Indeed, "there is no suffering which in this history of God is not God's suffering."[29]

By positing suffering as internal to the divine nature, thus entailing an eternal fissure in the divine life, we encounter not a God of genuine love who freely enters into covenant with creatures but a God who "loves" us as part of a divine self-realization project. As Eastern Orthodox theologian David Bentley Hart argues, if we require God to suffer in his own nature in order to be loving, "goodness then requires evil to be good; love must be goaded into being by pain. In brief, a God who can, in his nature as God, suffer cannot be the God who is love, even if at the end of the day he should prove to be loving, or the God who is simply good, or who is the wellspring of being and life."[30] Theologians such as Moltmann seem to be expositing the idea that "God is love" (1 John 4:8) without remembering that the same biblical book insists that this same God who is love is also "light and in him there is no darkness at all" (1 John 1:5). Indeed, as Gavrilyuk points out, in this view "the destructive nature of suffering is trivialized and falsely romanticized as something intrinsically valuable and redemptive."[31] Particularly in the midst of my own suffering, I have little patience with such romanticizing.

If the healing, Triune God, who has life in himself, is to rescue me from my despair, I need not only solidarity in my suffering; I also need to know that God's covenant love is so steady and powerful that suffering and death lose the finality of their poison because of Christ. Christ himself is that perfect medicine, for as the Son he is "the reflection of God's glory and the exact imprint of God's very being" (Heb. 1:3) and *also*, paradoxically, the pioneer who completes our salvation through suffering, our brother who also brings us into God's household as the Father's children. "It was fitting that God, for whom and through whom all things exist, in bringing many children to glory, should make the pioneer of their salvation perfect through sufferings. For the one who sanctifies and those who are sanctified all have one Father. For this reason Jesus is not ashamed to call them brothers and sisters" (Heb. 2:10–11). This God does not need suffering and death in order to be God, but in love that accords perfectly with his covenantal promises, God becomes incarnate in the Pioneer, our Brother, the great High Priest who is able to "sympathize with our weaknesses" in all of its humanity (Heb. 4:15). This is not "God against God." This is steadfast, trustworthy love.

Knowing a Love That Is beyond Knowledge

Several months after the transplant, as my time of "isolation" and quarantine was ending, I still felt beaten down. Emotionally, I felt raw and unstable—I did not want any more losses. I did not want to take risks. At times, I just felt alienated and misunderstood. "So, I hear you're doing really well!" "Are you feeling better every day?" "When will you be back to your old life?" All of the well-intentioned questions seemed to set me further back into the darkness—they seemed to obscure what I was going through rather than express it. I was doing well in some ways and very thankful for remission; but in other ways, I was not well. I was not feeling better each day. Sometimes I felt worse. And I would never return to my "old life."

When the doctor told me that I could return to public places, the first place I went was my local church congregation. I knew that I needed to be back in a place where I could join with others in feeding on the life-giving Christ through Word and sacrament. Moreover, their loving care was palpable and real, even when they didn't always say the "right things." Although I sometimes stammered and resisted as if I could reenter just fine on my own, they reminded me that "you will fulfill the law of Christ" when you "bear one another's burdens" (Gal. 6:2).

During this time, a small group from the church met with me for prayer, sharing, and theological reflection based on some common readings. In the midst of that prayer group, I started to see something strange happen: I was becoming more hopeful in my prayers at the same time that I was becoming less concerned that God follow my own plan and answer all of my specific requests in exactly the way that I was asking. Why? Because I was coming to realize that I can continue in prayer and hope because God is *not* an unjust judge but unspeakably generous (Luke 18:1–8). I was realizing that when I was feeling self-protective—unable to risk any more losses—I could rest in the love of God in Christ that was larger than even my prayers could comprehend. Paradoxically, Paul prays for the Ephesians that they "may have the power to comprehend" the "breadth and length and height and depth" (3:18) of Christ's love that "surpasses knowledge." In other words, God's love is not, thankfully, as frail as our love; it surpasses all of our calculations—we know it precisely when we know that we cannot truly measure its "breadth and length and height and depth." This is a covenant love that the psalmists trust in the midst of their anxiety, joy, anger, and misery. Indeed, it is the steadiness of God's covenant love that allows us to approach him in the unsteadiness of our frailty and anguish. This is the passionate love of God who "is able to accomplish abundantly far more than all we can ask or imagine" (Eph. 3:20). Precisely in coming to realize the depth of God's love in Christ that defied my calculation, I became increasingly open-handed in my prayers, hopeful in a generous and loving God—even when he didn't seem to follow the instructions of my (often banal) prayers. Very slowly, I started to reenter, like Job after his restoration, into the risks of loving others with awareness of the ongoing losses. To *know* that my comprehension of God's love in Christ was just the tip of the iceberg—to know that God is never an unjust judge, never asleep at the wheel—sent my calculating mind spinning. God is up to something bigger and better than my meager imagination realizes. This God who takes on our suffering in Christ in order to heal it is steady in his love even when I am not. This is the Lord, whose "steadfast love endures forever" (Ps. 136:1). The covenant Lord who promises this is faithful, steadfast, and unwavering. For as the book of Hebrews says after speaking about God's covenant promise to Abraham, God's loving promise is completely trustworthy. Unlike human beings who constantly toss and turn, fabricating and prevaricating about their promises, "it is impossible for God to lie" (Heb. 6:18 NIV).

10

"I Am Not My Own"

Our Story Incorporated into Christ's

"I am not my own, but belong—body and soul, in life and in death—to, my faithful Savior, Jesus Christ."[1] God and the story of his mighty acts and ongoing work are bigger than my cancer story. As I noted in the first chapter, God's story does not annihilate my cancer story, but it does envelop and redefine it. Indeed, it asks for my story to be folded into the dying and rising of Christ as one who belongs to him.

There are days I would prefer a different way. A less paradoxical route than the one this book has taken would have its advantages. "God just wants you to be healed!" "God's suffering with you—he couldn't do anything to prevent this tragedy!" "This [cancer] is just part of the perfect plan of God for your life!" These confidently spoken half-truths can never reach beyond half-truth because they are unwilling to face the biblical paradoxes inherent in orthodox Christianity. Such half-truths have always been a temptation because they present a path that is less formidable than fully belonging "body and soul, in life and in death—to Jesus Christ." Jesus Christ, the transcendent God incarnate, is the One through whom all things were made, yet he joins the psalmist in lamenting that this world of sin, suffering, and death is not the way things are supposed to be. Christ sometimes heals (in response to both belief and unbelief); at other times, he does not heal the physical ailments that seem so pressing to us. God is the sovereign King whose covenant love is absolutely steady; yet in this we again are left lamenting with the psalmist, for we don't know God's reasons for freely permitting a particular tragedy. Yet even when we feel left in the dark, even when suffering and death seem senseless, we are empowered by the Spirit to groan, lament, and yet rejoice. God's promise is trustworthy, and this same Spirit has united us to Christ, through whom we are able to call out to the Father as adopted children. We rejoice, we lament. In all of this, our own stories are not preserved in a pristine way; we are displaced ("I am not my own") and incorporated into a much larger story—God's story in Christ.

Several months before my transplant, I wrote the following as I anticipated test results about whether my cancer levels were sufficiently low after chemotherapy to receive a transplant.

Displacement and Psalm 27

> The LORD is my light and my salvation—
>> whom shall I fear?
> The LORD is the stronghold of my life—
>> of whom shall I be afraid? . . .
> One thing I ask from the LORD,
>> this only do I seek:
> that I may dwell in the house of the LORD
>> all the days of my life,
> to gaze on the beauty of the LORD
>> and to seek him in his temple." (Ps. 27:1, 4 NIV)

I returned to these verses on the night and morning before my meeting with the oncologist on Monday morning. They are not just words of reassurance but words of displacement. Why should I not be afraid? I may expect, hope, or think I "deserve" a positive outcome on my test results. I can rationalize my way into thinking that with the best in medical technology on my side, my future isn't as foggy as it seems. The list could go on. . . . As I revisited these verses, however, I could sense that my hopes, expectations, and various aspects of unbelief were being crowded out, displaced, by the word Yʜᴡʜ, "the Lᴏʀᴅ." The Lord—not my hope for good medical news—is my light and salvation. The Lord—not my trust in medical technology—is the stronghold of my life. Lest I had any doubt that the psalmist was bringing me this direction, verse 4 reminded me that there is "one thing I ask from the Lᴏʀᴅ, this only do I seek"—namely, dwelling in the house and temple of the Lord, being in his presence.

Humanly speaking, this process of displacement is impossible to complete on my own. I can't do it. But in prayer, I am assured by the fact that I don't pray alone. The Spirit prays in and through me (Rom. 8:15–16), displacing me by shifting my trust from myself to the Lord to whom I belong. Moreover, I pray this prayer of displacement as a disciple of Christ, as one who belongs to the living, reigning Christ. For disciples, this prayer of displacement in Psalm 27:1 merges into "Thy kingdom come, Thy will be done in earth, as it is in heaven." And this finds its culmination in Christ himself, who underwent the ultimate displacement for our sakes. "Father, if you are willing, take this cup from me; yet, not my will, but yours be done" (Luke 22:42). Maybe, hopefully, by the Spirit I can taste just a bit of that joyful displacement from self, sin, and unbelief, moving instead to the spacious place of trusting that the Lord is enough—the Lord, the God of Israel, made known in Christ, is enough on his own to counter our fears. Ultimately, the Lord is sufficient for calming my fears and needs no help from anything on my self-calming "list."

Taking It Slow with the Psalmist

God uses prayer that moves toward trust in his promises to change us. By the Spirit, God uses prayer with the self-presentation of Jesus Christ in Word and sacrament to incorporate us into Christ's story, where we belong. I've explored specific aspects of this in this book, particularly related to praying the Psalms. We don't have to suppress anger or confusion or misery before coming before the Almighty. With an open heart, we bring all of this before the covenant Lord, entrusting him to hear our cries and moving toward trust in his loving-faithfulness and covenant promises. Moreover, since we pray the Psalms with Christ and in Christ, all of our prayer resonates with the Lord's Prayer. "Thy kingdom come, Thy will be done." We ask God to "rule us by your Word and Spirit in such a way that more and more we submit to you."[2] As we pray this, we confess, "I am not my own";[3] we are displaced from our old self, which seeks autonomy, to find our true life in that of the crucified Lord, the One to whom the Spirit conforms us.

But this process of displacement of our old self and incorporation into Christ is a long journey. It is long because of the persistence of our sin, our love of life that moves away from God's ways and seeks out autonomy rather than communion with God and neighbor. But as I discovered anew during my time of recovery after the transplant, it is also a long journey because until the kingdom comes in its fullness, our lives will be ones of both rejoicing and lament before our covenant Lord.

So, I'm in remission! I am grateful to God. It reminds me of the psalms of thanksgiving, which recall the pleas to God that one cries out of "the Pit."

> To you, O LORD, I cried,
>> and to the LORD I made supplication:
> "What profit is there in my death,
>> if I go down to the Pit?

172

Will the dust praise you?

    Will it tell of your faithfulness?

Hear, O Lᴏʀᴅ, and be gracious to me!

    O Lᴏʀᴅ, be my helper!" (Ps. 30:8–10)

The verses following change tone dramatically, giving thanks for the Lord's deliverance.

You have turned my mourning into dancing;

    you have taken off my sackcloth

    and clothed me with joy,

so that my soul may praise you and not be silent.

    O Lᴏʀᴅ my God, I will give thanks to you forever.

      (Ps. 30:11–12)

There are certain aspects of this movement from "the Pit" to "thanksgiving" that are my prayer right now—overall, I continue to do "very well," by doctor's standards; I'm in remission. I genuinely and earnestly give thanks to God.

But if I am honest, I have to admit that's not the whole story about either my physical or emotional life right now. I am giving thanks and praising God but also still lamenting. Eugene Peterson notes that on the one hand, "most Psalms are complaints. They are calls of help by helpless and hurting men and women."[4] Yet many individual psalms (like Ps. 30), and the book of Psalms as a whole, end with exuberant praise. Even psalms of lament/complaint usually end with a word of trust in God's deliverance. Peterson says that the fact that the book of Psalms ends in praises indicates that "our prayers are going to end in praise, but that it is going to take a while. Don't rush it. It may take years, decades even, before certain prayers arrive at hallelujahs, at Psalms 146–150."[5] Don't rush it. If we short-circuit our continued pleas and laments, then we're hiding our hearts from God and can't fully enter into the thanksgiving and praise. I like those words: "Don't rush it." Take it slow. God is bigger than cancer and our other trials. And the final chapters of our prayers will be praise. But in the meantime, our lives are not so one-sided that we can leave behind the psalms of lament and just pray psalms of thanksgiving instead.

In Romans 12, Paul speaks about how Christians offer their lives to God as "living sacrifices" in gratitude; this includes living out the imperatives to "rejoice with those who rejoice; mourn with those who mourn." I've always thought of this as referring to ministry to two different sets of people—some who are rejoicing, others who are mourning. But I'm discovering that as a patient in remission from an incurable cancer that is expected to return, I'm both rejoicing and mourning at the same time.

Until the kingdom comes in its fullness, the Christian life will continue to involve ongoing lament and ongoing rejoicing. The Psalms are indispensable for this journey, for they focus our eyes on the covenant God and his promises amid the lament and rejoicing. And contrary to my own expectations, as ones who thank God for every good gift yet cry out, "Thy kingdom come," we should not expect the rejoicing and the lamenting to come from two separate groups of people.

Walking in the Way of the Cross: Discerning the Place of Suffering and Delight

Does this mean that Christians should seek out suffering? I have often heard preachers assure largely middle-class congregations that the answer to this question is no. And that answer is right, in a certain way and to a certain extent. God has created us to be creatures of delight—we need to learn to delight in God and his gifts, to celebrate his faithful provision. Faith itself, John Calvin says, involves "placing our love and delight" in God.[6] God is the Creator, the giver of many gifts, the giver of every breath and heartbeat. And God is not overtaken by even the tragedies that overtake us. We can and should delight in God's gifts, and we can even delight in the way that God brings good out of evil in our trials. This, among other things, frees us from taking ourselves too seriously. As creatures in the hands of God, we need to let laughter roll over us like a refreshing bath. On my fortieth birthday, my fatigue was still heavy, and I had to carefully ration my time around people to avoid complete exhaustion. But joining together with family and friends, we still celebrated. At the celebration, I unveiled a present for Neti to her great delight: a punk-rock style blue wig of hair. (When we had first told Neti that I would lose my hair, she had said that she hoped God would give me blue hair.) "Blue hair! Blue hair!" God has finally given Dada the blue hair Neti hoped for! (I only got to wear the wig a few minutes before Neti decided that *she* wanted to wear the blue hair!) Our house has had many squeals of delight and hearty laughter since my diagnosis.

And yet, while we should not seek suffering for its own sake, when we cry out, "Thy kingdom come," we are giving ourselves by the Spirit to Christ's cross-shaped kingdom. This is what is behind Paul's peculiar language about suffering. "I am now rejoicing in my sufferings for your sake" (Col. 1:24); "I want to know Christ and the power of his resurrection and the sharing of his sufferings by becoming like him in his death" (Phil. 3:10); "for while we live, we are always being given up to death for Jesus's sake, so that the life of Jesus may be made visible in our mortal flesh" (2 Cor. 4:11). Why would Paul speak this way? Because the gift of new life in union with Christ involves the gift of sharing in Christ's sufferings as part of the Spirit's work in conforming us to the crucified Lord. Indeed, as Michael Gorman notes about Romans 8:17, part of our identity as God's adopted children—on this side of the fullness of the kingdom—is to be "co-sufferers" with Christ. "If children, then heirs, heirs of God and joint heirs with Christ—if, in fact, we suffer with him [literally, "co-suffer"; Greek *sympaschomen*] so that we may also be glorified with him."[7] For Paul, life in union with Christ means that "suffering is somehow part of the grace of believing existence."[8] This should not surprise us. For Jesus says, "If any want to become my followers, let them deny themselves and take up their cross daily and follow me" (Luke 9:23).

Moreover, while we should not *seek* to suffer for its own sake, we need to take up our cross daily and not live in service to the affluent ideals of a consumer culture that has become expert at avoiding suffering. We need to join with the laments of Christ that declare that the suffering, injustice, and unbelief of our world are not the way things are supposed to be. We need to rediscover the cries of the suffering in the Psalms and ask for God to use those prayers to help us to become close to sufferers in our midst, saying, "Thy kingdom come." As Carl Trueman notes about the loss of the psalms of lament in Christian worship, "By excluding the cries of loneliness, dispossession, and desolation from its worship, the church has effectively silenced and excluded the voices of those who are themselves lonely, dispossessed, and desolate, both inside and outside the church. By doing so, it has implicitly endorsed the banal aspirations of consumerism."[9]

One gift that I have received from my cancer diagnosis is that friends in my midst have been especially open about times when they have faced suffering and trials—particularly relating to life-threatening illnesses. They have prayed for me, and they rightly think that it is quite natural for them to share their burdens with me also. They insist that my prayers and stumbling words are helpful. And in a strange way, I can welcome them into a place of lament with the psalmists; it is less lonely there when others are joining in the song. We give each other gifts.

Indeed, while Christians should not *seek suffering*, we should *seek out the suffering*. It's a part of our identity and calling, part of who we are as those who take up our crosses and as ones sent as Christ's witnesses into the world. We don't expect to "change the world" or to fix everyone's problems. But we seek to compassionately bear witness to Christ and his kingdom—this suffering, unbelief, and abuse is not the way things are supposed to be. As we do so, we are always receivers as well as givers. I recall many conversations with homeless men while I was on staff at a shelter in the Boston area. I was a doctoral student at Harvard at the time. The homeless men couldn't care less about that fact. They didn't care about the latest debates about postmodernism or epistemology. But in my encounters with them—with all of their virtues and vices, strengths and obvious challenges—I received just a bit of healing of my pride and freedom from some of my delusions. I also received the gift of learning to celebrate in some simple ways with them. I became known as the guy who would dare to use the oven (which had no temperature control!) to bake cakes to share. In the fourth century, Gregory of Nyssa described this mutual gift-giving in a vivid way. His congregation was afraid to serve those with leprosy for fear of the contagion. But in touching those wounds, Gregory argued, we can actually receive healing. "If we wish to heal the wounds by which our sins have afflicted us, heal today the ulcers which break down their flesh."[10]

A theology of the cross is not a joyless path but one with tears of joy and celebration as well as tears of lament. Lamenting with the psalmists is a practice that is counter to our consumer culture. Lament fixes our eyes on God's promises and brings the cries of confusion and pain—our own and those of others—before the covenant Lord. We also rejoice with the psalmists in God's many and lavish gifts, for every breath is a gift—and even though my cancer is in a very real sense "not the way things are supposed to be," God uses it as an occasion for giving gifts as well. Ultimately, as I take it slow with the psalmists, I still groan and ache. I lament deeply. But in the midst of being incorporated into Christ's cross-shaped path, there are also hallelujahs anticipating the praise of Psalms 146–50.

Calculating the New Life

Several months after my transplant, I sent out the following update in an attempt to give a window into the "new life" in which I found myself.

Life on Chemo, or Chemo for Life

A few days ago, I started on the "low dose" chemotherapy that I will need to stay on until the cancer returns. Hopefully, that will be years. So, I'm hoping and praying for a long remission, which also means

I'm hoping to be on this chemo for a long time. My jaw dropped at the price when it arrived by UPS: over $8,800 a month (pre-insurance). I'm thankful for God's provision for our family in health insurance, but it makes me distressed for those without it.

This chemotherapy is a pill that I take daily for three weeks out of every month; I will also have monthly visits to the cancer center to receive a bone strengthener by IV and testing to make sure that I'm still in remission.

As far as chemotherapy goes, this one usually has relatively few side effects. The biggest problem with it is that it is known to increase the risk for secondary cancers. But since my myeloma is expected to return, the risk of dying from myeloma is greater than the risk of developing other cancers. This underscores something that one of my doctors told me recently: being in remission is *not* a return to "the old life" before being diagnosed with the cancer. There is no return to the "old life." There is only the possibility of entering into a new one.

In another CarePages entry, I expanded on these aspects of the "new life" on chemo, giving some theological reflections as well.

Recently I was reading John Calvin's commentary on Psalm 52:8–9:

> But I am like a green olive tree
>   in the house of God.
> I trust in the steadfast love of God
>   forever and ever.
> I will thank you forever,
>   because of what you have done.
> In the presence of the faithful
>   I will proclaim your name, for it is good.

178

In meditating on the word "forever" in these verses, Calvin notes that the psalmist "would not presume to prescribe times to God, and that his hopes were stretched into eternity." Thus the psalmist "surrendered himself entirely to God in all that regarded this life or his death."[11] May it be so for us, as we praise, petition, lament, and bless God along the journey of life, thankful for each day as a gift. . . .

It has been quite a journey since the diagnosis in September. There has been about a month in the hospital and a cancer lodge; hundreds of pokes; many chemo appointments; and a lot of bills. (I recently received a bill for $78,000, pre-insurance, for just *some* of the medical expenses in the last few months.) And at the end of this part of the journey, I received good news about recovery and remission.

Yet there is still uncertainty about what will happen in the future. It makes all the more potent Calvin's words that we "would not presume to prescribe times to God." Certainly in lament and petition we have a few prescriptions regarding the timing of our finite lives that we would like to give; indeed, we should do so. But ultimately the God of eternity is worthy of our trust "forever and ever," whatever our prospects for the future.

I don't know what the future will hold, but from a statistical standpoint, it's likely that I will die several decades earlier than I would have without the myeloma. I've spent time "calculating" what this might mean for me, for my family, for my career. How can you plan and face the future with goals without some calculation? This is my new life. It is no use pretending that it is not here. When I take my regimen of pills four times a day, feel the daily pain of peripheral neuropathy in my feet, and give myself an injection every twelve hours, the reminders are real enough.

While I believe that we should receive each breath, each day, as a gift, I tend to be skeptical of those who quote verses like Psalm 90:12 to say that we need to pack as much as possible into each and every second: "Teach us to count our days that we may gain a wise heart." For prior to these words, the psalmist says,

> The days of our life are seventy years,
>   or perhaps eighty, if we are strong;
> even then their span is only toil and trouble;
>   they are soon gone, and we fly away. (90:10)

The "wisdom" of the psalmist doesn't seem to be that we need to become even more rigid with controlling our second-by-second schedule, clinging all the harder to each moment. Instead the psalmist contrasts our lives with God's eternity to show us how utterly short our lives are.

> Lord, you have been our dwelling place
>   in all generations.
> Before the mountains were brought forth,
>   or ever you had formed the earth and the world,
>   from everlasting to everlasting you are God.
>
> You turn us back to dust,
>   and say, "Turn back, you mortals."
> For a thousand years in your sight
>   are like yesterday when it is past,
>   or like a watch in the night. (90:1–4)

The medical world gives cancer patients number after number, statistic after statistic, so that a person's life span and quality can be somehow expected; inevitably, cancer patients like myself experience moments of envy toward those who have been given many years. The night before traveling to my parents' fiftieth wedding anniversary, I experienced a sharp sadness. What are the chances that I could possibly live long enough to share that much time with Rachel? What kind of long-shot possibilities do I have to see my own children as grown adults, perhaps even to see grandchildren?

180

Moving beyond Calculation

But the psalmist pushes us to move beyond calculation in thinking of our life spans. When viewing the short years of even a long human life in light of God's eternity, the comparisons between human life spans seem absurd. Reflecting on this Psalm, Calvin says, "Each man, when he compares himself with others, flatters himself that he will live to a great age. In short, men are so dull as to think that thirty years, or even a smaller number, are, as it were, an eternity."[12] To live thirty years longer *seems* like an eternity to a cancer patient like myself—we become practiced in comparing life spans after diagnosis like comparing trophies, but what is thirty years in relation to eternity? We somehow assume that God owes us a long life, but all human lives before death are "like yesterday when it is past" (Ps. 90:4)—already past, already a memory. Even if we "win" what seems like a game in the cancer community—decades of remission—life is short, and our mortality-denying ways of living are absurd. As Martin Luther notes in his commentary on Psalm 90:4, "Today a person dies who yesterday had hoped to live another forty or more years. Even if such a person had actually realized his hope, even then he would not abandon the desire for a still longer life."[13]

When doctors told me of my prospects for a life span much shorter than I anticipated, a part of me wanted to cling to my previous hopes and expectations—to shout, "No! How could this be?" I joined and continue to join the psalmist in lament and petition; I still lament sharply, particularly as I think about the effect that my death would have on my young children and my spouse. But slowly, my clinging to my previous expectations has been loosened as well. As I move with the lamenting psalmist toward trust in the Lord and his covenant promises, the trust directs my vision toward the truly central actor in the drama—the Triune God—and his ongoing work in the world. For some of us, when we think about the future, we tend to make plans and goals as if we were the central character in what is happening—as if we could track the progress of Christ's kingdom by looking at our day planners and year-by-year goals. For others of us, we act as if we have all the time in the world without painful prioritizing, deciding on a day-by-day basis what people and tasks to really give ourselves to in love. Either way, we tend to live in an illusion that the psalmist seeks to free us from by contrasting God's eternity with our short days. As Luther writes in his Psalms commentary, "Everyone organizes his plans and projects as though he were going to live forever," but this is an illusion, since "all the while death everywhere dogs our footsteps and is at all times our nearest neighbor."[14]

While death is the last enemy to be defeated, God's work is not cramped or constricted by a shorter life span. The everlasting God is the One who brings his kingdom in his time, and although God uses us toward that end, it is not according to our schedule. Our attempt to squeeze every second out of every day is vain if it's not entering into a much larger work—the ongoing work of God in the world.

> Unless the LORD builds the house,
>   those who build it labor in vain.
> Unless the LORD guards the city,
>   the guard keeps watch in vain.
> It is in vain that you rise up early
>   and go late to rest. (Ps. 127:1–2)

We can't force God's work into our calendar, into the ten- and twenty-year goals for our churches, colleges, and seminaries. We can only seek to participate in the eternal God's ongoing work as grateful children of the Father united to Christ by the Spirit.

And even this participation in God's ongoing work is on a cross-shaped path—one that is filled with joyful surprises, but one where God works through and in the midst of our weakness. I reflected on this in a CarePages entry during my time of recovery after the transplant while struggling with very heavy fatigue.

"My Grace Is Sufficient for You"

In 2 Corinthians, the apostle Paul speaks about how he prayed repeatedly to God for a "thorn in the flesh" to be taken from him. God

182

did not answer in the way that he desired. "Three times I appealed to the Lord about this, that it would leave me" (2 Cor. 12:8). But Paul, the apostle who speaks so eloquently about the resurrection and the way in which it has implications now for the Christian (1 Cor. 15; Rom. 6), saw that in the current time, the normative pattern for the church is the way of the cross. For the Lord "said to me, 'My grace is sufficient for you, for my power is made perfect in weakness.' There-fore I will boast all the more gladly about my weaknesses, so that Christ's power may rest on me" (2 Cor. 12:9 NIV).

I cannot and do not claim that my fatigue is really like Paul's "thorn in the flesh." If all goes well, my fatigue will lessen and my strength will increase in the coming months. There may be more parallels with my overall cancer diagnosis in the sense that no matter how long my remission is, I am told by doctors that I will always need to expect my cancer to return; it will be a poignant reminder of my mortality each time that I do a test to see whether the remission is continuing. Nevertheless, even with the fatigue, there are fragmen-tary moments when I sense that the Spirit is saying, "My grace is sufficient for you."

For better or worse, I tend to be a "self-starter," a very "productive" person who likes to pack his schedule and accomplish goals. Since my diagnosis in September, I have continued to make daily lists of what to accomplish—whom to see, what tasks to complete, and so on. But I am much less likely to successfully make it through my list. The fatigue slows me down and makes me much less productive. Although I know that my value before God does not come through how much I accomplish, a part of me wants to justify myself through being productive. It is not easy for me to let go of that, to hear, "My grace is sufficient for you, for my power is made perfect in weak-ness." I think I'm beginning to hear it, but I sense I will spend this lifetime with that promise gradually sinking in. . . .

Moments of Grace in Times of Alertness and Times of Fatigue

In the midst of this, there have been some moments of grace in times of alertness as well as times of fatigue. In times of alertness, I've found that I've been able to do some serious reading and also some academic writing. While these tasks require energy, I also find them energizing. They are a real gift.

In my times of fatigue, I often feel like I can't do much at all. In particular, around our two high-energy kids, it can easily feel overwhelming. Nevertheless, during alert and semi-alert times, I've had some great times with the kids in the last few weeks.

A few days ago, though, I was watching our three-year-old, Neti, and the heavy fatigue really hit. I had just finished reading her a story. Then, a cloud of fatigue came over me—I couldn't concentrate, I couldn't focus, and my energy was all gone. Yet Neti is a very high-energy three-year-old. What would happen?

Neti has also been making strides in learning the meaning of empathy in recent months. It often takes a quite humorous form: she pretends that she has had an imaginary life doing the same thing she sees you doing. So, while Rachel is changing Nathaniel's diaper, she will say, "When I was a mommy, I used to change diapers, too." A few days ago, she even started to do this with inanimate objects! "When I was a bag of popcorn, I used to go into the microwave. . . ."

On this occasion, after I explained that Dada was very tired, she did not continue to ask me to play or to do other things for her. She grabbed a blanket and cuddled up next to me on the couch. And she stayed there. In a moment when I felt like I was about to "fail" because I didn't have the energy to be a lively dad, there was a different result. "My grace is sufficient for you, for my power is made perfect in weakness."

The End of the Story: I Belong to Jesus Christ

What is the end of the story? Not just the end of my cancer story, but the story of being incorporated into Christ and the ongoing work of the Triune God? The words that I used when I shared my diagnosis give testimony to a truth strong enough to carry me to the final chapter: my "only comfort in life and in death" is that "I am not my own, but belong—body and soul, in life and in death—to my faithful Savior, Jesus Christ." The same reality of God's new creation, life in Christ, will continue into the next, flourishing and deepening in communion with God. As the Heidelberg Catechism states, "Even as I already now experience in my heart the beginning of eternal joy, so after this life I will have perfect blessedness such as no eye has seen, no ear has heard, no human heart has ever imagined: a blessedness in which to praise God forever."[15] The continuity between now and then is none other than our incorporation into the life in Christ. In the words of Paul, "For to me, to live is Christ and to die is gain." Yet "I am torn between the two: I desire to depart and be with Christ, which is better by far" (Phil. 1:21, 23 NIV). Thus, "to live is Christ" and to die is to "be with Christ." The privilege of fellowship with God in Christ carries through. Christ's righteousness will continue to be a glorious gift on the day of judgment (justification), and the Spirit-enabled delight of sharing in the holy love and life of the Triune God will reach its fullness (sanctification). It will all be in and through the Triune God made known in Jesus Christ, the One to whom we belong in life and in death. As John Calvin notes, God's redemption of the good but fallen creation brings glorified humanity to a higher state than that of the first Adam through the loving fellowship of the Trinity. For "by the power of his Spirit he [Christ] imparts to us his life and all the blessings he has received from the Father."[16]

Yet how can we know these things when death sometimes seems like the doorway to a world of the unknown, or no world at all? Here's a hint: we don't leave the psalmist behind. As theologian Anthony Thiselton wrote after his near-fatal stroke, Christian confession about the future is not based on speculation or "a hypothetical assertion about the future."[17] Admittedly, Christians sometimes fall into the trap of approaching God's future like it is just information to be controlled, categorized, and manipulated. But as Thiselton wisely acknowledges, "We may look beyond the present only on the basis of [God's] *promise*."[18] As we have seen, the psalms of lament, thanksgiving, and praise have all directed our hearts to God's promise; preaching, baptism, and the Lord's Supper all direct us to God's covenant promise; and what we confess about the future is in the mode of trust—trusting that God's covenant promises will reach their final culmination, not only in heaven but on earth as well. Only God can do this. And inherent in the promise itself is that it will be in and through Christ. Thus we cry, "Come, Lord Jesus!" (Rev. 22:20).

In this promise that we confess, God restores and renews the whole of creation as it bows at the feet of Jesus Christ. That is the final chapter. In the words of Reformed theologian Herman Bavinck,

> Someday Christ will return visibly and then cause the whole believing community—indeed, the whole world—to participate in his glory. Not only are believers changed after his likeness, but also "the whole creation itself will be set free from its bondage to decay and obtain the freedom of the glory of the children of God" (Rom. 8:21). Earth and heaven will be renewed so that justice will be at home in them. The heavenly Jerusalem, which is now above and was the model for the earthly Jerusalem, then comes down to earth.[19]

In affirming this, Bavinck is not forcing God's hand by postulating a universal salvation or insisting that hell is empty. Rather, he's putting the last judgment in its proper, penultimate context, confessing the final end toward which history is heading: that "at the name of Jesus every knee should bend, in heaven and on earth and under the earth, and every tongue should confess that Jesus Christ is Lord, to the glory of God the Father" (Phil. 2:10–11). That is the final chapter. "In the end, God will be recognized as God by all creatures, if not willingly then unwillingly."[20] And this will happen with Jesus Christ at the center. For "in the Son the world has its foundation and example, and therefore

186

it has in him its goal as well. It is created through him and for him as well (Col. 1:16)."²¹ Jesus Christ, the One through whom God freely created all things, is restoring the earth as the dwelling place of God,²² leading creatures toward a face-to-face knowledge of a particular kind of glory: "For it is the God who said, 'Let light shine out of darkness,' who has shone in our hearts to give the light of the knowledge of the glory of God in the face of Jesus Christ" (2 Cor. 4:6).

We will never "get over" the comfort and hope that our lives are found in none other than Jesus Christ. He is "the Alpha and the Omega, the first and the last, the beginning and the end" (Rev. 22:13); he's not a temporary stopgap measure to rescue us from our sin. Even being face-to-face with God will always and ultimately be to look "in the face of Jesus Christ"—for the Son is "the reflection of God's glory and the exact imprint of God's very being" (Heb. 1:3). By the Spirit, our vision of God's new creation right now is in the face of Jesus Christ, as children of the Father; in the words of John Owen (reflecting on 2 Cor. 4:6), at the final, beatific vision "the blessed and blessing sight which we shall have of God will always be 'in the face of Jesus Christ.'"²³ We never move beyond Christ—the one whom Paul desired to "be with" after death. And the effect of coming to know God's glory in the face of Christ will be as transforming then (in fullness) as it is now (in part): "the vision we shall have of the glory of Christ in heaven, and of the glory of . . . God in him, is perfectly and absolutely transforming. It doth change us wholly into the image of Christ."²⁴ Glorified humanity is glorified in Christ.

Does this final chapter mean that we will finally know the answers to our open questions about God's action amid tragedies? The culmination of Christ's kingdom in the end will make things right. But as we've explored in previous chapters, that does not imply that it is up to us to construct "theodicies" to explain exactly how this will take place. The heavenly multitude will rightly declare on that day, "Hallelujah! Salvation and glory and power to our God, for his judgments are true and just" (Rev. 19:1). But while Scripture testifies that God will make all things right in the final chapter, the Bible doesn't promise that the resurrected in glory will know all the answers to our present questions. Some of our questions may indeed find wondrous answers, but many of the questions that seem so important to us now may simply fade away into irrelevance in the emerging vision of the depth and breadth of the divine purpose fulfilled in Jesus Christ—the Lamb of God who sits on the kingly throne (Rev. 5:6–14). Moreover, even in the final chapter, we will still be creatures, and God will be God. Only God will know God as God. We will still be worshiping the Triune God as the illuminating source of all light and life, a mystery beyond ourselves. And as we lament and petition and hope in God's promise right now amid calamities that can seem senseless, we can join the psalmist in trust that God will make things right in a way that we can only faintly imagine now.

> Let the sea roar, and all that fills it;
>   the world and those who live in it.
> Let the floods clap their hands;
>   let the hills sing together for joy
> at the presence of the LORD, for he is coming
>   to judge the earth.
> He will judge the world with righteousness,
>   and the peoples with equity. (Ps. 98:7–9)

Until that day when we join the whole earth in a song of praise, we still focus on God's promise through lament and thanksgiving, petition and praise. Full justice and restoration have not yet come; the world has not yet been made right. And while we have real tastes of the new creation in Christ by the Spirit, we still wait with groaning for our adoption to come in fullness. We walk on a cross-shaped path with the psalmist and with our crucified Lord, and yet in the end we will reach the final chapters of the Psalms, joyfully singing, "Let everything that breathes praise the LORD! Praise the LORD!" (Ps. 150:6). Then our true story, our true life—which is none other than life in the living Christ—will no longer be hidden but unveiled. "When Christ who is your life is revealed, then you also will be revealed with him in glory" (Col. 3:4). Christ is our life now in hiddenness. And Christ will be our life then in open glory. It will be clear to all that God is bigger than cancer and all of our other calamities. Thus whether we find ourselves in the darkness of the present time or the glorious light of the coming age, this good news is enough to bring us through: "That I am not my own, but belong—body and soul, in life and in death—to my faithful Savior, Jesus Christ."[25] Amen.

Notes

Preface

1. http://www.carepages.com/carepages/ToddBillings.

2. Readers familiar with my previous works will be able to identify some ongoing theological interests that I further develop from earlier works—including issues related to the theological interpretation of Scripture (*The Word of God for the People of God*), union with Christ (*Union with Christ*) and the theology of Calvin and the later Reformed tradition (*Calvin, Participation, and the Gift* and *Calvin's Theology and Its Reception*). There are also new areas of focus, including a theological rendering of the Psalms—and of lament in particular—providence, divine impassibility, and more. For those who would like a sketch of the overall theological framework in which I work—which seeks to occupy the broad Catholic tradition in a Reformed way—I would recommend "Rediscovering the Catholic-Reformed Tradition for Today: A Biblical, Christ-Centered Vision for Church Renewal," in *Reformed Catholicity: The Promise of Retrieval for Theology and Biblical Interpretation*, ed. Michael Allen and Scott R. Swain (Grand Rapids: Baker Academic, 2015).

Chapter 1: Walking in the Fog

1. Heidelberg Catechism, Q and A 1, *OF*.

2. Siddhartha Mukherjee, *The Emperor of All Maladies: A Biography of Cancer* (New York: Scribner, 2010), 443.

3. Ibid., 444.

4. Ibid.

5. See Jon Levenson, *Resurrection and the Restoration of Israel: The Ultimate Victory of the God of Life* (New Haven: Yale University Press, 2006), chaps. 12–13; quotation from p. 180.

6. See W. H. Bellinger, *Psalms: A Guide to Studying the Psalter*, 2nd ed. (Grand Rapids: Baker Academic, 2012), 50. Bellinger classifies no fewer than sixty-seven psalms as psalms of lament.

7. See William Holladay, *The Psalms through Three Thousand Years: Prayer Book of a Cloud of Witnesses* (Minneapolis: Fortress, 1993), 161–90.

8. Athanasius, *On the Incarnation: The Treatise* De Incarnatione Verbi Dei, rev. ed., ed. and trans. Religious of C.S.M.V. (Crestwood, NY: St. Vladimir's Seminary Press, 1983), 103.

9. John Calvin, *Preface to the Psalms*, in CTS.

10. Dietrich Bonhoeffer, *Psalms: The Prayer Book of the Bible* (Minneapolis: Augsburg, 1970), 21.

11. Ibid., 20–21.

Chapter 2: Sorting through the Questions

1. Tim Chaffey, *God and Cancer: Finding Hope in the Midst of Life's Trials* (Maitland, FL: Xulon, 2009), 183.

2. For more on the question of theodicy as an "open question," see Daniel Castelo, *Theological Theodicy* (Eugene, OR: Cascade, 2012), 88–89. Castelo wisely suggests that we should keep "a holy, earnest, restless silence" on the theodicy question, refusing to resolve it by restricting the power of God or by saying "in a speculative manner what God cannot do in relation to healing and making right the world."

3. See Carol M. Bechtel, "Knowing Our Limits: Job's Wisdom on Worship," in *Touching the Altar: The Old Testament for Christian Worship* (Grand Rapids: Eerdmans, 2008), 180–211, for more on the book of Job as pointing to "*the limits of human wisdom*" (181, emphasis in original).

4. For a defense of this translation of Job 42:6, see Roland Murphy, *The Tree of Life: An Exploration of Biblical Wisdom Literature*, 3rd ed. (Grand Rapids: Eerdmans, 2002), 43–44; Ellen Davis, *Getting Involved with God: Rediscovering the Old Testament* (Cambridge, MA: Cowley, 2001), 140–41.

5. Bechtel, "Knowing Our Limits," 193.

6. Davis, *Getting Involved with God*, 122.

7. See Tremper Longman III, *Job*, Baker Commentary on the Old Testament Wisdom and Psalms (Grand Rapids: Baker Academic, 2012), 52, 82–83. Longman explains, "While many translations give the impression that 'the accuser' is Satan, known as 'the devil' in the NT, it is best to understand this creature as a member of God's assembly." For "heaven here is described on analogy with an ancient royal court. The King is meeting with and receiving reports from his agents. The accuser is described as one who roams and patrols the earth (1:7; 2:2), in other words—a spy in God's service" (52). Thus, ultimately, the accuser in Job is one of God's "angelic associates, who takes the position of the devil's advocate, so to speak, but not of Satan himself" (82).

8. Gerald Janzen, *At the Scent of Water: The Ground of Hope in the Book of Job* (Grand Rapids: Eerdmans, 2009), 55.

9. See Longman, *Job*, 67, 462.

10. James Reitman, *Unlocking Wisdom: Forming Agents of God in the House of Mourning* (Springfield, MO: 21st Century, 2008), 63.

11. Bechtel, "Knowing Our Limits," 190.

12. Fyodor Dostoevsky, *The Brothers Karamazov*, trans. Richard Pevear and Larissa Volokhonsky (New York: North Point, 1990), 243.

13. Ibid., 245.

14. Ibid.

15. See James Kugel, *In the Valley of the Shadow: On the Foundations of Religious Belief (and Their Connection to a Certain, Fleeting State of Mind)* (New York: Free Press, 2011), 148–52.

16. See Alvin Plantinga, *God, Freedom, and Evil* (Grand Rapids: Eerdmans, 1977), 27.

17. Dostoevsky, *Brothers Karamazov*, 589.

18. Albert Camus, *The Rebel: An Essay on Man in Revolt*, trans. Anthony Bower (New York: Vintage, 1997), 58.

19. George R. Beasley-Murray, *John*, Word Biblical Commentary (Nashville: Thomas Nelson, 1987), 97.

20. Mark Galli, *God Wins: Heaven, Hell, and Why the Good News Is Better Than Love Wins* (Carol Stream, IL: Tyndale, 2011), 148.

Chapter 3: Lamenting in Trust

1. For an excellent account of this aspect of Augustine's thought, see Brian Brock, "Augustine's Incitement to Lament, from the *Enarrationes in Psalmos*," in *Evoking Lament: A Theological Discussion*, ed. Brian Brock and Eva Harasta (London: T&T Clark, 2009), 183–203.

2. See John Witvliet, *Worship Seeking Understanding: Windows into Christian Practice* (Grand Rapids: Baker Academic, 2003), 210.

3. See Glenn Pemberton, *Hurting with God: Learning to Lament with the Psalms* (Abilene, TX: Abilene Christian University Press, 2012), 35–41.

4. Carl Trueman, "Tragic Worship," *First Things*, June/July 2013, 20.

5. John Calvin, commentary on Psalm 62:8, CTS.

6. I am indebted to the analysis of Rolf A. Jacobson and Karl N. Jacobson in this section from *Invitation to the Psalms* (Grand Rapids: Baker Academic, 2013), 42–46.

7. On this point, Walter Brueggemann notes four elements of complaint in the psalms of lament: "1. Things are not right in the present arrangement. 2. They need not stay this way but can be changed. 3. The speaker will not accept them in this way, for it is intolerable. 4. It is God's obligation to change things." Brueggemann, "The Costly Loss of Lament," *Journal for the Study of the Old Testament* 36 (1986): 62.

8. Ellen Davis, *Getting Involved with God: Rediscovering the Old Testament* (Cambridge, MA: Cowley, 2001), 21, emphasis in original.

9. John Calvin, commentary on Psalm 51:8, CTS.

10. Brevard Childs, *Exodus: A Commentary* (London: SCM, 1974), 76.

11. Apostles' Creed. For more on the way in which New Testament uses of lament involve an interplay of groaning and hope, see Markus Ohler, "To Mourn, Weep, Lament, and Groan: On the Heterogeneity of the New Testament Statements on Lament," in *Evoking Lament*, ed. Eva Harasta and Brian Brock (London: T&T Clark, 2009), 150–65.

12. Pemberton, *Hurting with God*, 170.

13. See Jacobson and Jacobson, *Invitation to the Psalms*, 152. See also Rolf A. Jacobson, "'The Faithfulness of the Lord Endures Forever': The Theological Witness of the Psalter," in *Soundings in the Theology of the Psalms: Perspectives and Methods in Contemporary Scholarship*, ed. Rolf A. Jacobson (Minneapolis: Fortress, 2011), 111–38.

14. See Jacobson, "Faithfulness of the Lord," 112–13.

15. See J. J. Scullion, "God: God in the Old Testament," in *The Anchor Bible Dictionary*, ed. D. N. Freedman (New York: Doubleday, 1992), 2:1046.

16. Jacobson and Jacobson, *Invitation to the Psalms*, 46–50.

17. Ibid., 56–60.

18. Miroslav Volf, *Exclusion and Embrace: A Theological Exploration of Identity, Otherness, and Reconciliation* (Nashville: Abingdon, 1996), 124, emphasis added.

19. Davis, *Getting Involved with God*, 28.

20. While there are many expositions of the covenantal dimensions of the identity of Jesus Christ, N. T. Wright provides a helpful account in *Climax of the Covenant: Christ and the Law in Pauline Theology* (Minneapolis: Fortress, 1992).

21. Augustine on Psalm 85:1, in Saint Augustine, *Expositions of the Psalms: 73–98*, trans. Maria Boulding (New York: New City Press, 2002), 4:220.

Chapter 4: Lamenting to the Almighty

1. Glenn Pemberton, *Hurting with God: Learning to Lament with the Psalms* (Abilene, TX: Abilene Christian University Press, 2012), 93.

2. Ibid., 102.

3. See James Kugel, *In the Valley of the Shadow: On the Foundations of Religious Belief (and Their Connection to a Certain, Fleeting State of Mind)* (New York: Free Press, 2011), 132–36.

4. See Pemberton, *Hurting with God*, 149–60. My section here is indebted to Pemberton's analysis.

5. See James Luther Mays, *Psalms* (Louisville: John Knox, 1994), 350–51.

6. "God, in His ordinary providence, maketh use of means, yet is free to work without, above, and against them, at His pleasure." Westminster Confession of Faith, 5:3, 1647.

7. John Calvin, *Treatises against the Anabaptists and against the Libertines*, ed. and trans. Benjamin Wirt Farley (Grand Rapids: Baker, 1982), 322.

8. Michael S. Horton, *The Christian Faith: A Systematic Theology for Pilgrims on the Way* (Grand Rapids: Zondervan, 2011), 356, 361.

9. Ibid., 361, 359.

10. Ibid., 356.

11. Thomas Aquinas, *Summa Theologica* I.83.1, trans. Fathers of the English Dominican Province, vol. 1 (New York: Benzinger Bros., 1948), 418.

12. In utilizing this distinction, I am disagreeing with John Calvin, who utilized the distinction between primary and secondary causality but not the distinction between God's active and permissive will. However, a broad range of Reformed confessions (including the Belgic Confession, the Canons of Dort, and the Westminster Standards) disagree with Calvin on this point as well, utilizing the active/permissive distinction, though in a way that avoided suggesting that God is passive in his permissive will, the "bare permission" that the Westminster Confession warns against (Article 5:4). Thus, on this point, I align with the Reformed confessions in affirming a more "catholic" account of providence than Calvin.

13. Matthew Levering, *Predestination: Biblical and Theological Paths* (Oxford: Oxford University Press, 2011), 191.

14. The Reformed Bremen Consensus (1595), quoted in Jan Rohls, *Reformed Confessions* (Louisville: Westminster John Knox, 1998), 62–63. When confessions from the Reformation use the term "ordained" in this sense, it should not be construed in a monocausal way. God the King "ordains" through means (secondary causality), and this "ordaining" or willing may be active or permissive.

15. Heidelberg Catechism, Q and A 1, *OF*.

16. For an exploration of how these two claims can be held together with theological coherence, see *Reformed Thought on Freedom: The Concept of Free Choice in Early Modern Reformed Theology*, ed. Willem J. van Asselt, J. Martin Bac, and Roelf T. te Velde (Grand Rapids: Baker Academic, 2010), 110–14.

Chapter 5: Joining the Resistance

1. Karl Barth, *The Christian Life: Church Dogmatics,* IV/4, trans. Geoffrey Bromiley (Grand Rapids: Eerdmans, 1981), 168, 173.

2. Ibid., 211.

3. Ibid., 207, 212.

4. By speaking about our fallen world as "not the way things are supposed to be," I am not suggesting that the world is governed by chance. Rather, I give a dialectic framing for that phrase: "although the world is in God's hands, things are not the way they are supposed to be." Our present world is not the philosopher's dream of the "best of all possible worlds." God is king, and the creation is good; but the creation is also corrupted, turned in upon itself rather than oriented toward communion with God and God's ways. For an account of sin as a departure from "the way things are supposed to be," see Cornelius Plantinga, *Not the Way It's Supposed to Be: A Breviary of Sin* (Grand Rapids: Eerdmans, 1995), 14.

5. N. T. Wright, *The Case for the Psalms: Why They Are Essential* (New York: Harper-One, 2013), 139–40.

6. For an overview of a growing body of literature by biblical scholars and theologians who see dangers in claiming a "theoretical" answer to the theodicy question rather than focusing on a practical response to evils around us, see Daniel Castelo, *Theological Theodicy* (Eugene, OR: Cascade, 2012), esp. 1–30, 88–102.

7. Friedrich Nietzsche, *The Gay Science*, trans. Walter Kaufmann (New York: Vintage, 1974), 167.

8. Friedrich Nietzsche, *Thus Spoke Zarathustra*, in *The Portable Nietzsche*, trans. Walter Kaufmann (New York: Penguin, 1982), 439.

9. Ibid., 434.

10. Ibid., 434, 377.

11. Ross Gregory Douthat, *Bad Religion: How We Became a Nation of Heretics* (New York: Free Press, 2012), 235.

12. Christian Smith and Patricia Snell Herzog, *Souls in Transition: The Religious and Spiritual Lives of Emerging Adults* (Oxford: Oxford University Press, 2009), 68.

13. Christian Smith, Kari Marie Christoffersen, Hilary Davidson, and Patricia Snell Herzog, *Lost in Transition: The Dark Side of Emerging Adulthood* (New York: Oxford University Press, 2011), 108–9.

14. Ibid., 11.

15. Christian Smith and Melinda Lundquist Denton, *Soul Searching: The Religious and Spiritual Lives of American Teenagers* (New York: Oxford University Press, 2005), 162–63.

16. Ibid., 165.

17. Ibid.

18. The Reformed Bremen Consensus (1595), quoted in Jan Rohls, *Reformed Confessions* (Louisville: Westminster John Knox, 1998), 62–63.

19. For more on the way in which the attempt for a theoretical answer to the theodicy question is a distinctively Enlightenment and post-Enlightenment project, see Terrence W. Tilley, *The Evils of Theodicy* (Washington, DC: Georgetown University Press, 1991), 113–40, 221–55; Stanley Hauerwas, *God, Medicine, and Suffering* (Grand Rapids: Eerdmans, 1994), 51–53; David B. Burrell, *Deconstructing Theodicy: Why Job Has Nothing to Say to the Puzzle of Suffering* (Grand Rapids: Brazos, 2008), 107–38.

20. John Sanders, *The God Who Risks: A Theology of Divine Providence* (Downers Grove, IL: IVP Academic, 2007), 262.

21. Ibid.

22. See ibid., 15–38. This move influences his theological method, which minimizes the analogical distinction between God and humanity, interpreting anthropomorphisms in a more literal fashion. It also impacts his doctrine of God—downplaying classical notions of divine mystery and infinity, along with divine knowledge and power.

23. Ibid., 255, 262. It is important to note that when Sanders argues against a "specific sovereignty model," he mischaracterizes it as a functionally monocausal view—a view that classical Christian theology, including classical Reformed theology, explicitly denies. This takes place in his conceptual analysis (211–13) as well as in serious misinterpretations of pastoral situations. For example, Sanders recalls a graveside service with a pastor's speaking of "taking her [a little girl] home." "Of course, 'taking her home' is a euphemism for God's killing her" (10). While it is possible that the pastor held a monocausal view, the phrase "taking her home" need not imply that her death was a direct and immediate act of God, thus "God's killing her." Rather, it could be a way to express that even her death was not by chance but in God's hands, even if we don't know why God would permit secondary agents to act in a way that led to her death. In examples like this, Sanders repeatedly presents a false choice between open theism and a monocausal view of providence that sees every event as directly and immediately caused by God.

24. N. T. Wright, *Evil and the Justice of God* (Downers Grove, IL: InterVarsity, 2006), 59.

25. Ibid., 55, emphasis in original.

26. Ibid.

27. See Thomas C. Oden, *The Living God* (San Francisco: Harper & Row, 1987), 279–94, 300–302; Matthew Levering, *Predestination: Biblical and Theological Paths* (Oxford: Oxford University Press, 2011), 188–92; David Bentley Hart, *The Doors of the Sea: Where Was God in the Tsunami?* (Grand Rapids: Eerdmans, 2005), 86–87; Michael S. Horton, *The Christian Faith: A Systematic Theology for Pilgrims on the Way* (Grand Rapids: Zondervan, 2011), 358–59. In Hart, the distinction between God's (active) will and God's permission is especially key, contra John Calvin (see Hart, *Doors of the Sea*, 82–87, 90–91). (The other three theologians above utilize the distinction as well.) However, Hart does not note that the major Reformed confessions, such as the Belgic Confession, the Canons of Dort, and the Westminster Standards, agree with and utilize this distinction, contra Calvin. On the classical distinction, Hart writes, "The distinction is neither illogical nor slight; it is an absolute necessity if—setting aside, as we should, all other judgments as suppositious, stochastic, and secondary—we are to be guided by the full character of what is revealed of God in Christ. For, after all, if it is from Christ that we are to learn how God relates himself to sin, suffering, evil, and death, it would seem that he provides us little evidence of anything other than a regal, relentless, miraculous enmity: suffering he heals, evil he casts out, and death he conquers." Hart, *Doors of the Sea*, 86–87.

28. John K. Roth, "Theodicy of Protest," in *Encountering Evil: Live Options in Theodicy*, ed. Stephen T. Davis (Louisville: Westminster John Knox, 2001), 11.

29. Ibid.

30. C. S. Lewis, *A Grief Observed* (New York: Seabury, 1961), 37.

31. Roth, "Theodicy of Protest," 14.

32. Ibid., 36.

33. See James Kugel, *In the Valley of the Shadow: On the Foundations of Religious Belief (and Their Connection to a Certain, Fleeting State of Mind)* (New York: Free Press, 2011), 1–17.

34. John Calvin, commentary on Psalm 25:20, CTS.

Chapter 6: Death in the Story of God and in the Church

1. N. T. Wright, *Evil and the Justice of God* (Downers Grove, IL: InterVarsity, 2006), 19.

2. John Calvin, *Inst.*, 1.5.1.

3. In chaps. 4–5, I have utilized classical doctrinal categories in speaking about divine providence. As a supplement to these categories, I also draw upon the dramatic analogy of author, character, and narrative in this chapter. For a scholarly exposition of the usefulness of these categories as a way to testify to divine sovereignty and human freedom, see Kevin Vanhoozer, *Remythologizing Theology: Divine Action, Passion, and Authorship* (Cambridge: Cambridge University Press, 2010), 297–386.

4. Graham Swift, *Waterland* (London: Pan, 1992), 63.

5. See John Calvin's commentary on Genesis 2:9; 3:22, CTS. For more on this point, see J. Todd Billings, *Union with Christ: Reframing Theology and Ministry for the Church* (Grand Rapids: Baker Academic, 2011), 112–14.

6. Sermon by Jon Brown, "Reconciled," Pillar Church, Holland, Michigan, October 7, 2012.

7. Thomas Long, *The Good Funeral: Death, Grief, and the Community of Care* (Louisville: Westminster John Knox, 2013), 46.

8. Carl R. Trueman, "Tragic Worship," *First Things*, June/July 2013, 20.

9. Quoted in ibid., 20.

10. John L. Thompson, "An Exhortation to Martyrdom" (Pasadena, CA: Fuller Theological Seminary, 1997), 3, http://documents.fuller.edu/sot/faculty/thompson_john/Exhortation.pdf.

11. Ibid., 3–4.

12. Ibid., 4.

Chapter 7: Praying for Healing and Praying for the Kingdom

1. Heidelberg Catechism, Q and A 125, *OF*.

2. Gerhard Forde and Martin Luther, *On Being a Theologian of the Cross: Reflections on Luther's Heidelberg Disputation, 1518* (Grand Rapids: Eerdmans, 1997), 9.

3. Miltinnie Yih, "God's Role in My Son's Autism," *DTS Magazine*, July 3, 2013, http://www.dts.edu/read/gods-role-in-my-sons-autism/.

4. "If there is even hope in such a case [as the widow petitioning the unjust judge], then how much better must it be when we are dealing with the God of all goodness, and when the petitioner is one of God's own elect to whom he is deeply committed. God will certainly act for those of his own people who steadily look to him for the vindication of all that they stand for as his people." John Nolland, *Luke 9:21–18:34*, Word Biblical Commentary (Dallas: Word, 1993), 871. For more on the way in which this parable "is not about the power of repetitive prayer to move God," see David Crump, *Knocking on Heaven's Door: A New Testament Theology of Petitionary Prayer* (Grand Rapids: Baker Academic, 2006), 77–89.

5. In the words of Kevin Vanhoozer, prayer "is an asking in response to a prior divine communicative act: God's covenantal promise to be our God." Vanhoozer, *Remythologizing Theology: Divine Action, Passion, and Authorship* (Cambridge: Cambridge University Press, 2010), 379.

6. C. S. Lewis, "Petitionary Prayer: A Problem Without an Answer," in *Christian Reflections*, ed. Walter Hooper (Grand Rapids: Eerdmans, 2003), 144.

7. Augustine, comments on Psalm 102:5, in *Augustine in His Own Words*, trans. William Harmless (Washington, DC: Catholic University of America Press, 2010), 141.

8. Crump, *Knocking on Heaven's Door*, 43.

9. Ibid.

10. Ibid., 45.

11. As Crump points out, with Jesus's "stilling of the storm," his "feedings of the multitudes," and his "walking on water," the "evangelists make it clear that Jesus performed these miracles *in spite of* the disciples' *lack of faith*." See ibid., 43–44.

12. This is particularly evident in the Gospel of John. See ibid., 44–45.

13. Although I think that Lewis portrays more of a logical contradiction than a truly eschatological tension in this essay, he nevertheless explored the themes of prayer and healing with great insight, particularly in his works of fiction. See Alan Jacobs, *The Narnian: The Life and Imagination of C. S. Lewis* (San Francisco: HarperSanFrancisco, 2005), 4–9, for a lucid portrayal of Lewis's thought on this point.

14. Donald A. Hagner, *Matthew 14–28*, Word Biblical Commentary (Dallas: Word, 1995), 606.

15. N. T. Wright, *The Lord and His Prayer* (Grand Rapids: Eerdmans, 1997), 67.

16. S. E. Dowd, *Prayer, Power, and the Problem of Suffering: Mark 11:22–25 in the Context of Markan Theology* (Atlanta: Scholars Press, 1988), 158. Reflecting on Gethsemane in Mark's Gospel, Dowd notes that "the God who wills to move the mountain does not always will to take away the cup."

17. Martin Luther, *LW*, 31:53.

18. N. T. Wright, *Lord and His Prayer*, 75.

19. Ibid., 30.

Chapter 8: In the Valley

1. For an overview of the New Testament use of Psalm 69, see James Luther Mays, *Psalms*, Interpretation (Louisville: John Knox Press, 1994), 229–33.

2. Quoted in Augustine, *Augustine in His Own Words*, trans. William Harmless (Washington, DC: Catholic University of America Press, 2010), 142.

3. Quoted in ibid., 143.

4. John Calvin, commentary on Psalm 118:18, CTS.

5. When Paul speaks about the church as "the body of Christ," this is one of the ways he speaks about the corporate union of Christians with Christ and with one another—with Christians as subordinate under Christ the head, and interdependent in function. When the language is altered in order to speak about Christians as the "hands and feet" of Jesus in outreach, it actually moves against Paul's strong emphasis upon Christ as the "head of the body" in lordship over the church, "so that in everything he might have the supremacy" (Col. 1:18 NIV). For more on this cluster of theological issues, see J. Todd Billings, *Union with Christ: Reframing Theology and Ministry for the Church* (Grand Rapids: Baker Academic, 2011), chap. 5.

6. John Calvin, *Inst.*, 3.11.1.

7. Ibid., 3.11.2.

8. Ibid., 3.3.9.

9. For an illuminating treatment of this contrast in tenses for Paul on union with Christ, see Herman N. Ridderbos, *Paul: An Outline of His Theology* (Grand Rapids: Eerdmans, 1997), 253–58.

10. Luther, *LW*, 12:264.

11. Ibid., 12:260.

12. Calvin, commentary on Romans 6:5, CTS.

13. Calvin, *Inst.*, 3.11.

14. Luther, *LW*, 8:7.

15. Calvin, in his commentary on Psalm 103:3, CTS, refers to the gifts of justification and sanctification as God's "medicine."

Chapter 9: The Light of Perfect Love in the Darkness

1. Ellen Davis, *Getting Involved with God: Rediscovering the Old Testament* (Cambridge, MA: Cowley, 2001), 112.

2. Ibid., 141–42.

3. See Kelly Kapic, "Psalm 22: Forsakenness and the God Who Sings," in *Theological Commentary: Evangelical Perspectives*, ed. R. Michael Allen (London: T&T Clark, 2011), 42.

4. John Calvin, commentary on Psalm 88:14, CTS.

5. See Kapic, "Psalm 22," 53.

6. Indeed, this hope is particularly emphasized in Luke's Gospel, where Christ's cry from Ps. 22 is followed by an explicit declaration of trust from another psalm of lament—Ps. 31:5: "Into your hands, I commit my spirit." In Christ's quotation of this psalm, his declaration of trust is further expressed by addressing God as "Father" (Luke 23:46).

7. Heidelberg Catechism, Q and A 44, OF.

8. Ambrose, *Exposition of the Christian Faith*, in *St. Ambrose: Selected Works and Letters*, trans. H. de Romestin (Grand Rapids: Eerdmans, 1998), 230.

9. This definitional issue is quite important—for as Kevin Vanhoozer states, contemporary theologians "tend to hear 'incapable of experiencing emotions'" when they approach impassibility, but that is not implied by the classic definitions. Vanhoozer, *Remythologizing Theology: Divine Action, Passion, and Authorship* (Cambridge: Cambridge University Press, 2010), 397. See also the helpful historical survey of Rob Lister, which shows how the mainstream, historic tradition of divine impassibility does *not* assert that God is incapable of affections. Lister, *God Is Impassible and Impassioned: Toward a Theology of Divine Emotion* (Wheaton: Crossway, 2013), chaps. 2–4.

10. Lister, *God Is Impassible and Impassioned*, 36, emphasis in original.

11. Sometimes theologians debate about whether these terms are "mere anthropomorphisms." I think scriptural language about God's emotions is anthropomorphic, but there is nothing "mere" about such a rendering. Scriptural language about God's emotions consists of *God-given* anthropomorphisms—God-given in revelation as the most faithful way that we can come to speak of, sing of, and know God and his ways. Indeed, with Herman Bavinck, I would insist that "Scripture does not contain just a few scattered anthropomorphisms but is anthropomorphic through and through." Bavinck, *Reformed Dogmatics*, vol. 2, *God and Creation*, trans. John Vriend, ed. John Bolt (Grand Rapids: Baker Academic, 2004), 99. Yet they are "not arbitrary" or "conceived by us at our own pleasure" (99) but are precious gifts given in loving, divine accommodation to our weakness. For more on this point, see J. Todd Billings, *Union with Christ: Reframing Theology and Ministry for the Church* (Grand Rapids: Baker Academic, 2011), chap. 3.

12. For an illuminating contrast between God's jealousy and human jealousy, see Vanhoozer, *Remythologizing Theology*, 414–16.

13. Thomas McCall, *Forsaken: The Trinity and the Cross, and Why It Matters* (Downers Grove, IL: IVP Academic, 2012), 70.

14. See Paul Gavrilyuk, *The Suffering of the Impassible God: The Dialectics of Patristic Thought* (New York: Oxford University Press, 2004), 38–39, 101–71.

15. Richard Muller, *Post-Reformation Reformed Dogmatics*, vol. 3, *The Rise and Development of Reformed Orthodoxy, ca. 1520 to ca. 1725* (Grand Rapids: Baker Academic, 2003), 33.

16. "There is but one only, living, and true God, who is infinite in being and perfection, a most pure spirit, invisible, *without* body, parts, or *passions*; immutable, immense, eternal, incomprehensible, almighty, most wise, most holy, most free, most absolute; working all things according to the counsel of His own immutable and most righteous will, for His own glory; *most loving, gracious, merciful, long-suffering, abundant in goodness and truth, forgiving iniquity, transgression, and sin; the rewarder of them that diligently seek Him; and withal, most just, and terrible in His judgments, hating all sin, and who will by no means clear the guilty.*" Westminster Confession of Faith (2.1), emphasis added. While the Westminster Confession explicitly affirms impassibility, in the Reformed tradition in particular, the doctrinal elements of divine impassibility have often been affirmed as a part of a doctrine of immutability. Historically, impassibility and immutability are very closely related on a conceptual level, and "immutability" is the more common term in the Reformed confessions and in the Reformed scholastic treatments. See Muller, *Post-Reformation Reformed Dogmatics*, 3:308–20.

17. Gavrilyuk, *The Suffering of the Impassible God*, 62.

18. Thomas Weinandy, *Does God Suffer?* (Notre Dame: University of Notre Dame Press, 2000), 126–27.

19. See Elaine Scarry, *The Body in Pain* (Oxford: Oxford University Press, 1987), esp. 3–26, quotation from p. 3.

20. Theologians call this way of speech the "communication of idioms." While accounts of the theological significance of this speech varies, the Council of Chalcedon affirms it as a way to assert the full unity of Jesus Christ; and historic expressions of Roman Catholic, Orthodox, and most Protestant theologies affirm its usage as well.

21. St. Gregory of Nazianzus, *On God and Christ: The Five Theological Orations and Two Letters to Cledonius*, trans. Frederick Williams (Crestwood, NY: St. Vladimir's Seminary Press, 2002), 86.

22. Ibid., 158, 88, 111.

23. Council of Chalcedon, "Definition of Faith," in *Decrees of the Ecumenical Councils*, ed. Norman P. Tanner (London: Sheed and Ward, 1990), 1:85–86.

24. Paul Gavrilyuk, "God's Impassible Suffering in the Flesh: The Promise of Paradoxical Christology," in *Divine Impassibility and the Mystery of Human Suffering*, ed. James F. Keating and Thomas Joseph White (Grand Rapids: Eerdmans, 2009), 148.

25. Jürgen Moltmann, *The Crucified God: The Cross of Christ as the Foundation and Criticism of Christian Theology* (New York: Harper & Row, 1974), 152.

26. William Stacy Johnson, "Jesus' Cry, God's Cry, and Ours," in *Lament: Reclaiming Practices in Pulpit, Pew, and Public Square*, ed. Sally A. Brown and Patrick D. Miller (Louisville: Westminster John Knox, 2005), 84.

27. Moltmann, *Crucified God*, 244.

28. For an overview of the key passages in Moltmann on this point, see John Cooper, *Panentheism—The Other God of the Philosophers: From Plato to the Present* (Grand Rapids: Baker Academic, 2006), 241–58.

29. Moltmann, *Crucified God*, 146.

30. David B. Hart, "No Shadow of Turning: On Divine Impassibility," *Pro Ecclesia* 11, no. 2 (Spring 2002): 191.

31. Gavrilyuk, "God's Impassible Suffering," 145.

Chapter 10: "I Am Not My Own"

1. Heidelberg Catechism, Q and A 1, *OF*.
2. Heidelberg Catechism, Q and A 123, *OF*.

3. Heidelberg Catechism, Q and A 1, *OF.*

4. Eugene Peterson, *Answering God: The Psalms as Tools for Prayer* (San Francisco: Harper & Row, 1989), 121.

5. Ibid., 127.

6. John Calvin, commentary on Psalm 91:14–15, CTS.

7. Michael Gorman, *Cruciformity: Paul's Narrative Spirituality of the Cross* (Grand Rapids: Eerdmans, 2001), 385.

8. Ibid., 301.

9. Carl Trueman, "What Can Miserable Christians Sing?," in *The Wages of Spin: Critical Writings on Historic and Contemporary Evangelicalism* (Fearn, UK: Mentor, 2004), 160.

10. Gregory of Nyssa, "On the Saying, 'Whoever Has Done It to One of These Has Done It to Me,'" trans. Susan R. Holman in the appendix of *The Hungry Are Dying: Beggars and Bishops in Roman Cappadocia* (New York: Oxford University Press, 2001), 205.

11. Calvin, commentary on Psalm 52:8–9, CTS.

12. Calvin, commentary on Psalm 90:4, CTS.

13. Luther, *LW*, 13:100.

14. Ibid.

15. Heidelberg Catechism, Q and A 58, *OF.*

16. Calvin, commentary on John 17:21, CTS.

17. Anthony Thiselton, *Life after Death: A New Approach to the Last Things* (Grand Rapids: Eerdmans, 2012), 16, 26.

18. Ibid., 20.

19. Herman Bavinck, *Reformed Dogmatics*, vol. 4, *Holy Spirit, Church, and New Creation*, trans. John Vriend, ed. John Bolt (Grand Rapids: Baker Academic, 2008), 719. Note: a listing of Bible references as source texts has been removed from this quotation for brevity.

20. Ibid., 4:713.

21. Ibid., 4:685.

22. On the way in which Gen. 1 portrays the created cosmos as the dwelling place of God—a cosmic temple—see John Walton, *The Lost World of Genesis One: Ancient Cosmology and the Origins Debate* (Downers Grove, IL: IVP Academic, 2009).

23. John Owen, *Meditations and Discourses on the Glory of Christ* (New York: Robert Carter, 1839), 292–93. For a superb exposition of Owen's account of the beatific vision, see Suzanne McDonald, "Beholding the Glory of God in the Face of Jesus Christ: John Owen and the 'Reforming' of the Beatific Vision," in *The Ashgate Research Companion to John Owen's Theology*, ed. Mark Jones and Kelly M. Kapic (Burlington, VT: Ashgate, 2012), 141–58.

24. Owen, *Meditations*, 410, emphasis in original.

25. Heidelberg Catechism, Q and A 1, *OF.*